EVERYMAN,
I WILL GO WITH THEE
AND BE THY GUIDE,
IN THY MOST NEED
TO GO BY THY SIDE

D0090309

EVERYMAN'S LIBRARY
POCKET POETS

Auden

Poems

Selected by
Edward Mendelson

EVERYMAN'S LIBRARY

POCKET POETS

Alfred A. Knopf · New York · Toronto

Typography by Peter B. Willberg

Typeset in the UK by MS Filmsetting Ltd., Frome, Somerset

Printed and bound in Germany
by Graphischer Großbetrieb Pößneck GmbH

W. H. AUDEN

CONTENTS

TALLER TO-DAY

Taller to-day, we remember similar evenings,
Walking together in a windless orchard
Where the brook runs over the gravel, far from the
$$\qquad\qquad\qquad\qquad\text{glacier.}$$

Nights come bringing the snow, and the dead howl
Under headlands in their windy dwelling
Because the Adversary put too easy questions
On lonely roads.

But happy now, though no nearer each other,
We see farms lighted all along the valley;
Down at the mill-shed hammering stops
And men go home.

Noises at dawn will bring
Freedom for some, but not this peace
No bird can contradict: passing but here, sufficient now
For something fulfilled this hour, loved or endured.

THE SECRET AGENT

Control of the passes was, he saw, the key
To this new district, but who would get it?
He, the trained spy, had walked into the trap
For a bogus guide, seduced by the old tricks.

At Greenhearth was a fine site for a dam
And easy power, had they pushed the rail
Some stations nearer. They ignored his wires:
The bridges were unbuilt and trouble coming.

The street music seemed gracious now to one
For weeks up in the desert. Woken by water
Running away in the dark, he often had
Reproached the night for a companion
Dreamed of already. They would shoot, of course,
Parting easily two that were never joined.

THIS LUNAR BEAUTY

This lunar beauty
Has no history,
Is complete and early;
If beauty later
Bear any feature
It had a lover
And is another.

This like a dream
Keeps other time,
And daytime is
The loss of this;
For time is inches
And the heart's changes
Where ghost has haunted,
Lost and wanted.

But this was never
A ghost's endeavour
Nor, finished this,
Was ghost at ease;
And till it pass
Love shall not near
The sweetness here
Nor sorrow take
His endless look.

THE QUESTION

To ask the hard question is simple:
Asking at meeting
With the simple glance of acquaintance
To what these go
And how these do;
To ask the hard question is simple,
The simple act of the confused will.

But the answer
Is hard and hard to remember:
On steps or on shore
The ears listening
To words at meeting,
The eyes looking
At the hands helping,
Are never sure
Of what they learn
From how these things are done,
And forgetting to listen or see
Makes forgetting easy,
Only remembering the method of remembering,
Remembering only in another way,
Only the strangely exciting lie,
Afraid

To remember what the fish ignored,
How the bird escaped, or if the sheep obeyed.

Till, losing memory,
Bird, fish, and sheep are ghostly,
And ghosts must do again
What gives them pain.
Cowardice cries
For windy skies,
Coldness for water,
Obedience for a master.
Shall memory restore
The steps and the shore,
The face and the meeting place;
Shall the bird live,
Shall the fish dive,
And sheep obey
In a sheep's way;
Can love remember
The question and the answer,
For love recover
What has been dark and rich and warm all over?

WHAT'S IN YOUR MIND, MY DOVE,
MY CONEY

What's in your mind, my dove, my coney;
Do thoughts grow like feathers, the dead end of life;
Is it making of love or counting of money,
Or raid on the jewels, the plans of a thief?

Open your eyes, my dearest dallier;
Let hunt with your hands for escaping me;
Go through the motions of exploring the familiar;
Stand on the brink of the warm white day.

Rise with the wind, my great big serpent;
Silence the birds and darken the air;
Change me with terror, alive in a moment;
Strike for the heart and have me there.

'O WHERE ARE YOU GOING?'

'O where are you going?' said reader to rider,
'That valley is fatal where furnaces burn,
Yonder's the midden whose odours will madden,
That gap is the grave where the tall return.'

'O do you imagine,' said fearer to farer,
'That dusk will delay on your path to the pass,
Your diligent looking discover the lacking,
Your footsteps feel from granite to grass?'

'O what was that bird,' said horror to hearer,
'Did you see that shape in the twisted trees?
Behind you swiftly the figure comes softly,
The spot on your skin is a shocking disease.'

'Out of this house' – said rider to reader,
'Yours never will' – said farer to fearer,
'They're looking for you' – said hearer to horror,
As he left them there, as he left them there.

THE WANDERER

Doom is dark and deeper than any sea-dingle.
Upon what man it fall
In spring, day-wishing flowers appearing,
Avalanche sliding, white snow from rock-face,
That he should leave his house,
No cloud-soft hand can hold him, restraint by women;
But ever that man goes
Through place-keepers, through forest trees,
A stranger to strangers over undried sea,
Houses for fishes, suffocating water,
Or lonely on fell as chat,
By pot-holed becks
A bird stone-haunting, an unquiet bird.

There head falls forward, fatigued at evening,
And dreams of home,
Waving from window, spread of welcome,
Kissing of wife under single sheet;
But waking sees
Bird-flocks nameless to him, through doorway voices
Of new men making another love.

Save him from hostile capture,
From sudden tiger's leap at corner;
Protect his house,
His anxious house where days are counted
From thunderbolt protect,
From gradual ruin spreading like a stain;
Converting number from vague to certain,
Bring joy, bring day of his returning,
Lucky with day approaching, with leaning dawn.

ADOLESCENCE

By landscape reminded once of his mother's figure
The mountain heights he remembers get bigger
                                    and bigger:
With the finest of mapping pens he fondly traces
All the family names on the familiar places.

In a green pasture straying, he walks by still waters;
Surely a swan he seems to earth's unwise daughters,
Bending a beautiful head, worshipping not lying,
'Dear' the dear beak in the dear concha crying.

Under the trees the summer bands were playing;
'Dear boy, be brave as these roots,' he heard them saying:
Carries the good news gladly to a world in danger,
Is ready to argue, he smiles, with any stranger.

And yet this prophet, homing the day is ended,
Receives odd welcome from the country he so defended:
The band roars 'Coward, Coward,' in his human fever,
The giantess shuffles nearer, cries 'Deceiver'.

HAVE A GOOD TIME

'We have brought you,' they said, 'a map of the country;
Here is the line that runs to the vats,
This patch of green on the left is the wood,
We've pencilled an arrow to point out the bay.
No thank you, no tea; why look at the clock.
Keep it? Of course. It goes with our love.

'We shall watch your future and send our love.
We lived for years, you know, in the country.
Remember at week-ends to wind up the clock.
We've wired to our manager at the vats.
The tides are perfectly safe in the bay,
But whatever you do don't go to the wood.

'There's a flying trickster in that wood,
And we shan't be there to help with our love.
Keep fit by bathing in the bay,
You'll never catch fever then in the country.
You're sure of a settled job at the vats
If you keep their hours and live by the clock.'

He arrived at last; it was time by the clock.
He crossed himself as he passed the wood;
Black against evening sky the vats
Brought tears to his eyes as he thought of their love;
Looking out over the darkening country,
He saw the pier in the little bay.

At the week-ends the divers in the bay
Distracted his eyes from the bandstand clock;
When down with fever and in the country
A skein of swans above the wood
Caused him no terror; he came to love
The moss that grew on the derelict vats.

And he has met sketching at the vats
Guests from the new hotel in the bay;
Now, curious, following his love,
His pulses differing from the clock,
Finds consummation in the wood
And sees for the first time the country.

Sees water in the wood and trees by the bay,
Hears a clock striking near the vats:
'This is your country and the hour of love'.

A SUMMER NIGHT
(to Geoffrey Hoyland)

Out on the lawn I lie in bed,
Vega conspicuous overhead
   In the windless nights of June,
As congregated leaves complete
Their day's activity; my feet
   Point to the rising moon.

Lucky, this point in time and space
Is chosen as my working-place,
   Where the sexy airs of summer,
The bathing hours and the bare arms,
The leisured drives through a land of farms
   Are good to a newcomer.

Equal with colleagues in a ring
I sit on each calm evening
   Enchanted as the flowers
The opening light draws out of hiding
With all its gradual dove-like pleading,
   Its logic and its powers:

That later we, though parted then,
May still recall these evenings when
    Fear gave his watch no look;
The lion griefs loped from the shade
And on our knees their muzzles laid,
    And Death put down his book.

Now north and south and east and west
Those I love lie down to rest;
    The moon looks on them all,
The healers and the brilliant talkers,
The eccentrics and the silent walkers,
    The dumpy and the tall.

She climbs the European sky,
Churches and power-stations lie
    Alike among earth's fixtures:
Into the galleries she peers
And blankly as a butcher stares
    Upon the marvellous pictures.

To gravity attentive, she
Can notice nothing here, though we
    Whom hunger does not move,
From gardens where we feel secure
Look up and with a sigh endure
    The tyrannies of love:

And, gentle, do not care to know,
Where Poland draws her eastern bow,
    What violence is done,
Nor ask what doubtful act allows
Our freedom in this English house,
    Our picnics in the sun.

Soon, soon, through dykes of our content
The crumpling flood will force a rent
    And, taller than a tree,
Hold sudden death before our eyes
Whose river dreams long hid the size
    And vigours of the sea.

But when the waters make retreat
And through the black mud first the wheat
    In shy green stalks appears,
When stranded monsters gasping lie,
And sounds of riveting terrify
    Their whorled unsubtle ears,

May these delights we dread to lose,
This privacy, need no excuse
    But to that strength belong,
As through a child's rash happy cries
The drowned parental voices rise
    In unlamenting song.

After discharges of alarm
All unpredicted let them calm
    The pulse of nervous nations,
Forgive the murderer in his glass,
Tough in their patience to surpass
    The tigress her swift motions.

PAYSAGE MORALISÉ

Hearing of harvests rotting in the valleys,
Seeing at end of street the barren mountains,
Round corners coming suddenly on water,
Knowing them shipwrecked who were launched
                                    for islands,
We honour founders of these starving cities
Whose honour is the image of our sorrow,

Which cannot see its likeness in their sorrow
That brought them desperate to the brink of valleys;
Dreaming of evening walks through learned cities
They reined their violent horses on the mountains,
Those fields like ships to castaways on islands,
Visions of green to them who craved for water.

They built by rivers and at night the water
Running past windows comforted their sorrow;
Each in his little bed conceived of islands
Where every day was dancing in the valleys
And all the green trees blossomed on the mountains,
Where love was innocent, being far from cities.

But dawn came back and they were still in cities;
No marvellous creature rose up from the water;
There was still gold and silver in the mountains
But hunger was a more immediate sorrow,
Although to moping villagers in valleys
Some waving pilgrims were describing islands ...

'The gods,' they promised, 'visit us from islands,
Are stalking, head-up, lovely, through our cities;
Now is the time to leave your wretched valleys
And sail with them across the lime-green water,
Sitting at their white sides, forget your sorrow,
The shadow cast across your lives by mountains.'

So many, doubtful, perished in the mountains,
Climbing up crags to get a view of islands,
So many, fearful, took with them their sorrow
Which stayed them when they reached unhappy cities,
So many, careless, dived and drowned in water,
So many, wretched, would not leave their valleys.

It is our sorrow. Shall it melt? Then water
Would gush, flush, green these mountains
                                  and these valleys,
And we rebuild our cities, not dream of islands.

O WHAT IS THAT SOUND

O what is that sound which so thrills the ear
    Down in the valley drumming, drumming?
Only the scarlet soldiers, dear,
    The soldiers coming.

O what is that light I see flashing so clear
    Over the distance brightly, brightly?
Only the sun on their weapons, dear,
    As they step lightly.

O what are they doing with all that gear,
    What are they doing this morning, this morning?
Only their usual manoeuvres, dear,
    Or perhaps a warning.

O why have they left the road down there,
    Why are they suddenly wheeling, wheeling?
Perhaps a change in their orders, dear.
    Why are you kneeling?

O haven't they stopped for the doctor's care,
    Haven't they reined their horses, their horses?
Why, they are none of them wounded, dear,
    None of these forces.

O is it the parson they want, with white hair,
    Is it the parson, is it, is it?
No, they are passing his gateway, dear,
    Without a visit.

O it must be the farmer who lives so near.
    It must be the farmer so cunning, so cunning?
They have passed the farmyard already, dear,
    And now they are running.

O where are you going? Stay with me here!
    Were the vows you swore deceiving, deceiving?
No, I promised to love you, dear,
    But I must be leaving.

O it's broken the lock and splintered the door,
    O it's the gate where they're turning, turning;
Their boots are heavy on the floor
    And their eyes are burning.

OUR HUNTING FATHERS

Our hunting fathers told the story
　　Of the sadness of the creatures,
Pitied the limits and the lack
　　Set in their finished features;
Saw in the lion's intolerant look,
Behind the quarry's dying glare,
Love raging for the personal glory
　　That reason's gift would add,
The liberal appetite and power,
　　The rightness of a god.

Who, nurtured in that fine tradition,
　　Predicted the result,
Guessed Love by nature suited to
　　The intricate ways of guilt,
That human ligaments could so
His southern gestures modify
And make it his mature ambition
　　To think no thought but ours,
To hunger, work illegally,
　　And be anonymous?

WHO'S WHO

A shilling life will give you all the facts:
How Father beat him, how he ran away,
What were the struggles of his youth, what acts
Made him the greatest figure of his day:
Of how he fought, fished, hunted, worked all night,
Though giddy, climbed new mountains; named a sea:
Some of the last researchers even write
Love made him weep his pints like you and me.

With all his honours on, he sighed for one
Who, say astonished critics, lived at home;
Did little jobs about the house with skill
And nothing else; could whistle; would sit still
Or potter round the garden; answered some
Of his long marvellous letters but kept none.

MAY

May with its light behaving
Stirs vessel, eye and limb,
The singular and sad
Are willing to recover,
And to each swan-delighting river
The careless picnics come
In living white and red.

Our dead, remote and hooded,
In hollows rest, but we
From their vague woods have broken,
Forests where children meet
And the white angel-vampires flit,
Stand now with shaded eye,
The dangerous apple taken.

The real world lies before us,
Brave motions of the young,
Abundant wish for death,
The pleasing, pleasured, haunted:
A dying Master sinks tormented
In his admirers' ring,
The unjust walk the earth.

And love that makes impatient
Tortoise and roe, that lays
The blonde beside the dark,
Urges upon our blood,
Before the evil and the good
How insufficient is
Touch, endearment, look.

ON THIS ISLAND

Look, stranger, on this island now
The leaping light for your delight discovers,
Stand stable here
And silent be,
That through the channels of the ear
May wander like a river
The swaying sound of the sea.

Here at a small field's ending pause
Where the chalk wall falls to the foam and its tall ledges
Oppose the pluck
And knock of the tide,
And the shingle scrambles after the suck-
-ing surf, and a gull lodges
A moment on its sheer side.

Far off like floating seeds the ships
Diverge on urgent voluntary errands,
And this full view
Indeed may enter
And move in memory as now these clouds do,
That pass the harbour mirror
And all the summer through the water saunter.

NIGHT MAIL
(Commentary for a G.P.O. Film)

I

This is the Night Mail crossing the Border,
Bringing the cheque and the postal order,

Letters for the rich, letters for the poor,
The shop at the corner, the girl next door.

Pulling up Beattock, a steady climb:
The gradient's against her, but she's on time.

Past cotton-grass and moorland boulder,
Shovelling white steam over her shoulder,

Snorting noisily, she passes
Silent miles of wind-bent grasses.

Birds turn their heads as she approaches,
Stare from the bushes at her blank-faced coaches.

Sheep-dogs cannot turn her course;
They slumber on with paws across.

In the farm she passes no one wakes,
But a jug in a bedroom gently shakes.

II

Dawn freshens. Her climb is done.
Down towards Glasgow she descends,
Towards the steam tugs yelping down a glade of cranes,
Towards the fields of apparatus, the furnaces
Set on the dark plain like gigantic chessmen.
All Scotland waits for her:
In dark glens, beside pale-green lochs,
Men long for news.

III

Letters of thanks, letters from banks,
Letters of joy from girl and boy,
Receipted bills and invitations
To inspect new stock or to visit relations,
And applications for situations,
And timid lovers' declarations,
And gossip, gossip from all the nations,
News circumstantial, news financial,
Letters with holiday snaps to enlarge in,
Letters with faces scrawled on the margin,
Letters from uncles, cousins and aunts,
Letters to Scotland from the South of France,
Letters of condolence to Highlands and Lowlands,
Written on paper of every hue,
The pink, the violet, the white and the blue,

The chatty, the catty, the boring, the adoring,
The cold and official and the heart's outpouring,
Clever, stupid, short and long,
The typed and the printed and the spelt all wrong.

IV

Thousands are still asleep,
Dreaming of terrifying monsters
Or a friendly tea beside
            the band in Cranston's or Crawford's:
Asleep in working Glasgow,
                  asleep in well-set Edinburgh,
Asleep in granite Aberdeen,
They continue their dreams,
But shall wake soon and hope for letters,
And none will hear the postman's knock
Without a quickening of the heart.
For who can bear to feel himself forgotten?

AS I WALKED OUT ONE EVENING

As I walked out one evening,
    Walking down Bristol Street,
The crowds upon the pavement
    Were fields of harvest wheat.

And down by the brimming river
    I heard a lover sing
Under an arch of the railway:
    'Love has no ending.

'I'll love you, dear, I'll love you
    Till China and Africa meet,
And the river jumps over the mountain
    And the salmon sing in the street,

'I'll love you till the ocean
    Is folded and hung up to dry
And the seven stars go squawking
    Like geese about the sky.

'The years shall run like rabbits,
    For in my arms I hold
The Flower of the Ages,
    And the first love of the world.'

But all the clocks in the city
    Began to whirr and chime:
'O let not Time deceive you,
    You cannot conquer Time.

'In the burrows of the Nightmare
    Where Justice naked is,
Time watches from the shadow
    And coughs when you would kiss.

'In headaches and in worry
    Vaguely life leaks away,
And Time will have his fancy
    To-morrow or to-day.

'Into many a green valley
    Drifts the appalling snow;
Time breaks the threaded dances
    And the diver's brilliant bow.

'O plunge your hands in water,
    Plunge them in up to the wrist;
Stare, stare in the basin
    And wonder what you've missed.

'The glacier knocks in the cupboard,
    The desert sighs in the bed,
And the crack in the tea-cup opens
    A lane to the land of the dead.

'Where the beggars raffle the banknotes
    And the Giant is enchanting to Jack,
And the Lily-white Boy is a Roarer,
    And Jill goes down on her back.

'O look, look in the mirror,
    O look in your distress;
Life remains a blessing
    Although you cannot bless.

'O stand, stand at the window
    As the tears scald and start;
You shall love your crooked neighbour
    With your crooked heart.'

It was late, late in the evening,
    The lovers they were gone;
The clocks had ceased their chiming,
    And the deep river ran on.

THE DREAM

Dear, though the night is gone,
Its dream still haunts to-day,
That brought us to a room
Cavernous, lofty as
A railway terminus,
And crowded in that gloom
Were beds, and we in one
In a far corner lay.

Our whisper woke no clocks,
We kissed and I was glad
At everything you did,
Indifferent to those
Who sat with hostile eyes
In pairs on every bed,
Arms round each other's necks,
Inert and vaguely sad.

What hidden worm of guilt
Or what malignant doubt
Am I the victim of,
That you, then, unabashed,
Did what I never wished,
Confessed another love;
And I, submissive, felt
Unwanted and went out.

FISH IN THE UNRUFFLED LAKES

Fish in the unruffled lakes
Their swarming colours wear,
Swans in the winter air
A white perfection have,
And the great lion walks
Though his innocent grove;
Lion, fish and swan
Act, and are gone
Upon Time's toppling wave.

We, till shadowed days are done,
We must weep and sing
Duty's conscious wrong,
The Devil in the clock,
The goodness carefully worn
For atonement or for luck;
We must lose our loves,
On each beast and bird that moves
Turn an envious look.

Sighs for folly done and said
Twist our narrow days,
But I must bless, I must praise
That you, my swan, who have
All gifts that to the swan
Impulsive Nature gave,
The majesty and pride,
Last night should add
Your voluntary love.

AUTUMN SONG

Now the leaves are falling fast,
Nurse's flowers will not last,
Nurses to their graves are gone,
But the prams go rolling on.

Whispering neighbours left and right
Daunt us from our true delight,
Able hands are forced to freeze
Derelict on lonely knees.

Close behind us on our track,
Dead in hundreds cry Alack,
Arms raised stiffly to reprove
In false attitudes of love.

Scrawny through a plundered wood,
Trolls run scolding for their food,
Owl and nightingale are dumb,
And the angel will not come.

Clear, unscaleable, ahead
Rise the Mountains of Instead,
From whose cold cascading streams
None may drink except in dreams.

UNDERNEATH AN ABJECT WILLOW

Underneath an abject willow,
    Lover, sulk no more:
Act from thought should quickly follow.
    What is thinking for?
Your unique and moping station
    Proves you cold;
    Stand up and fold
Your map of desolation.

Bells that toll across the meadows
    From the sombre spire
Toll for these unloving shadows
    Love does not require.
All that lives may love; why longer
    Bow to loss
    With arms across?
Strike and you shall conquer.

Geese in flocks above you flying,
    Their direction know,
Icy brooks beneath you flowing,
    To their ocean go.
Dark and dull is your distraction:
    Walk then, come,
    No longer numb
Into your satisfaction.

AT LAST THE SECRET IS OUT

At last the secret is out, as it always must come in the end,
The delicious story is ripe to tell to the intimate friend;
Over the tea-cups and in the square the tongue has
                           its desire;
Still waters run deep, my dear, there's never smoke
                              without fire.

Behind the corpse in the reservoir, behind the ghost on
                            the links,
Behind the lady who dances and the man who madly
                             drinks,
Under the look of fatigue, the attack of migraine and
                            the sigh
There is always another story, there is more than
                            meets the eye.

For the clear voice suddenly singing, high up in the
                            convent wall,
The scent of the elder bushes, the sporting prints in
                            the hall,
The croquet matches in summer, the handshake, the
                         cough, the kiss,
There is always a wicked secret, a private reason for this.

FUNERAL BLUES

Stop all the clocks, cut off the telephone,
Prevent the dog from barking with a juicy bone,
Silence the pianos and with muffled drum
Bring out the coffin, let the mourners come.

Let aeroplanes circle moaning overhead
Scribbling on the sky the message He Is Dead,
Put crêpe bows round the white necks of the public
                                          doves,
Let the traffic policemen wear black cotton gloves.

He was my North, my South, my East and West,
My working week and my Sunday rest,
My noon, my midnight, my talk, my song;
I thought that love would last for ever: I was wrong.

The stars are not wanted now: put out every one;
Pack up the moon and dismantle the sun;
Pour away the ocean and sweep up the wood;
For nothing now can ever come to any good.

JOHNNY

O the valley in the summer where I and my John
Beside the deep river would walk on and on
While the flowers at our feet and the birds up above
Argued so sweetly on reciprocal love,
And I leaned on his shoulder; 'O Johnny, let's play':
But he frowned like thunder and he went away.

O that Friday near Christmas as I well recall
When we went to the Charity Matinee Ball,
The floor was so smooth and the band was so loud
And Johnny so handsome I felt so proud;
'Squeeze me tighter, dear Johnny, let's dance till it's day':
But he frowned like thunder and he went away.

Shall I ever forget at the Grand Opera
When music poured out of each wonderful star?
Diamonds and pearls they hung dazzling down
Over each silver or golden silk gown;
'O John I'm in heaven,' I whispered to say:
But he frowned like thunder and he went away.

O but he was as fair as a garden in flower,
As slender and tall as the great Eiffel Tower,
When the waltz throbbed out on the long promenade
O his eyes and his smile they went straight to my heart;
'O marry me, Johnny, I'll love and obey':
But he frowned like thunder and he went away.

O last night I dreamed of you, Johnny, my lover,
You'd the sun on one arm and the moon on the other,
The sea it was blue and the grass it was green,
Every star rattled a round tambourine;
Ten thousand miles deep in a pit there I lay:
But you frowned like thunder and you went away.

ROMAN WALL BLUES

Over the heather the wet wind blows,
I've lice in my tunic and a cold in my nose.

The rain comes pattering out of the sky,
I'm a Wall soldier, I don't know why.

The mist creeps over the hard grey stone,
My girl's in Tungria; I sleep alone.

Aulus goes hanging around her place,
I don't like his manners, I don't like his face.

Piso's a Christian, he worships a fish;
There'd be no kissing if he had his wish.

She gave me a ring but I diced it away;
I want my girl and I want my pay.

When I'm a veteran with only one eye
I shall do nothing but look at the sky.

O TELL ME THE TRUTH ABOUT LOVE

Some say that love's a little boy,
      And some say it's a bird,
Some say it makes the world go round,
      And some say that's absurd,
And when I asked the man next-door,
      Who looked as if he knew,
His wife got very cross indeed,
      And said it wouldn't do.

    Does it look like a pair of pyjamas,
      Or the ham in a temperance hotel?
    Does its odour remind one of llamas,
      Or has it a comforting smell?
    Is it prickly to touch as a hedge is,
      Or soft as eiderdown fluff?
    Is it sharp or quite smooth at the edges?
      O tell me the truth about love.

Our history books refer to it
      In cryptic little notes,
It's quite a common topic on
      The Transatlantic boats;

I've found the subject mentioned in
      Accounts of suicides,
And even seen it scribbled on
      The backs of railway-guides.

    Does it howl like a hungry Alsatian,
      Or boom like a military band?
    Could one give a first-rate imitation
      On a saw or a Steinway Grand?
    Is its singing at parties a riot?
      Does it only like Classical stuff?
    Will it stop when one wants to be quiet?
      O tell me the truth about love.

I looked inside the summer-house;
      It wasn't ever there:
I tried the Thames at Maidenhead,
      And Brighton's bracing air.
I don't know what the blackbird sang,
      Or what the tulip said;
But it wasn't in the chicken-run,
      Or underneath the bed.

Can it pull extraordinary faces?
  Is it usually sick on a swing?
Does it spend all its time at the races,
  Or fiddling with pieces of string?
Has it views of its own about money?
  Does it think Patriotism enough?
Are its stories vulgar but funny?
  O tell me the truth about love.

When it comes, will it come without warning
  Just as I'm picking my nose?
Will it knock on my door in the morning,
  Or tread in the bus on my toes?
Will it come like a change in the weather?
  Will its greeting be courteous or rough?
Will it alter my life altogether?
  O tell me the truth about love.

CASINO

Only their hands are living, to the wheel attracted,
are moved, as deer trek desperately towards a creek
   through the dust and scrub of a desert, or gently,
      as sunflowers turn to the light,

and, as night takes up the cries of feverish children,
the cravings of lions in dens, the loves of dons,
   gathers them all and remains the night, the
      great room is full of their prayers.

To a last feast of isolation self-invited,
they flock, and in a rite of disbelief are joined;
   from numbers all their stars are recreated,
      the enchanted, the worldly, the sad.

Without, calm rivers flow among the wholly living
quite near their trysts, and mountains part them,
                                             and birds,
   deep in the greens and moistures of summer,
      sing towards their work.

But here no nymph comes naked to the youngest
                                    shepherd,
the fountain is deserted, the laurel will not grow;
    the labyrinth is safe but endless, and broken
        is Ariadne's thread,

as deeper in these hands is grooved their fortune: lucky
were few, and it is possible that none was loved,
    and what was god-like in this generation
        was never to be born.

DOVER

Steep roads, a tunnel through chalk downs,
                              are the approaches;
A ruined pharos overlooks a constructed bay;
The sea-front is almost elegant; all the show
Has, inland somewhere, a vague and dirty root:
        Nothing is made in this town.

A Norman castle, dominant, flood-lit at night,
Trains which fume in a station built on the sea,
Testify to the interests of its regular life:
Here dwell the experts on what the soldiers want,
        And who the travellers are

Whom ships carry in or out between the lighthouses,
Which guard for ever the made privacy of this bay
Like twin stone dogs opposed on a gentleman's gate.
Within these breakwaters English is properly spoken,
        Outside an atlas of tongues.

The eyes of departing migrants are fixed on the sea,
Conjuring destinies out of impersonal water:
'I see an important decision made on a lake,
An illness, a beard, Arabia found in a bed,
        Nanny defeated, Money.'

Red after years of failure or bright with fame,
The eyes of homecomers thank these historical cliffs:
'The mirror can no longer lie nor the clock reproach;
In the shadow under the yew, at the children's party,
     Everything must be explained.'

The Old Town with its Keep and Georgian houses
Has built its routine upon such unusual moments;
Vows, tears, emotional farewell gestures,
Are common here, unremarkable actions
     Like ploughing or a tipsy song.

Soldiers crowd into the pubs in their pretty clothes,
As pink and silly as girls from a high-class academy;
The Lion, The Rose, The Crown, will
                      not ask them to die,
Not here, not now: all they are killing is time,
     A pauper civilian future.

Above them, expensive, shiny as a rich boy's bike,
Aeroplanes drone through the new European air
On the edge of a sky that makes England of minor
                           importance;
And tides warn bronzing bathers of a cooling star
     With half its history done.

High over France, a full moon, cold and exciting
Like one of those dangerous flatterers we meet and love
When we are utterly wretched, returns our stare:
The night has found many recruits; to
                                    thousands of pilgrims
      The Mecca is coldness of heart.

The cries of the gulls at dawn are sad like work:
The soldier guards the traveller who pays for
                                        the soldier,
Each prays in a similar way for himself, but neither
Controls the years or the weather. Some may be heroes:
      Not all of us are unhappy.

DEATH'S ECHO

'O who can ever gaze his fill,'
    Farmer and fisherman say,
'On native shore and local hill,
 Grudge aching limb or callus on the hand?
 Father, grandfather stood upon this land,
 And here the pilgrims from our loins will stand.'
    So farmer and fisherman say
    In their fortunate hey-day:
 But Death's low answer drifts across
 Empty catch or harvest loss
    Or an unlucky May.
 The earth is an oyster with nothing inside it,
    Not to be born is the best for man;
 The end of toil is a bailiff's order,
    Throw down the mattock and dance while you can.

'O life's too short for friends who share,'
    Travellers think in their hearts,
'The city's common bed, the air,
 The mountain bivouac and the bathing beach,
 Where incidents draw every day from each
 Memorable gesture and witty speech.'
    So travellers think in their hearts,
    Till malice or circumstance parts
 Them from their constant humour:

And slyly Death's coercive rumour
    In that moment starts.
A friend is the old old tale of Narcissus,
    Not to be born is the best for man;
An active partner in something disgraceful,
    Change your partner, dance while you can.

'O stretch your hands across the sea,'
    The impassioned lover cries,
'Stretch them towards your harm and me.
Our grass is green, and sensual our brief bed,
The stream sings at its foot, and at its head
The mild and vegetarian beasts are fed.'
    So the impassioned lover cries
    Till the storm of pleasure dies:
From the bedpost and the rocks
Death's enticing echo mocks,
    And his voice replies.
The greater the love, the more false to its object,
    Not to be born is the best for man;
After the kiss comes the impulse to throttle,
    Break the embraces, dance while you can.

'I see the guilty world forgiven,'
    Dreamer and drunkard sing,
'The ladders let down out of heaven,
The laurel springing from the martyr's blood,

The children skipping where the weeper stood,
The lovers natural and the beasts all good.'
    So dreamer and drunkard sing
    Till day their sobriety bring:
Parrotwise with Death's reply
From whelping fear and nesting lie,
    Woods and their echoes ring.
The desires of the heart are as crooked as corkscrews,
    Not to be born is the best for man;
The second-best is a formal order,
    The dance's pattern; dance while you can.
Dance, dance, for the figure is easy,
    The tune is catching and will not stop;
Dance till the stars come down from the rafters;
    Dance, dance, dance till you drop.

LULLABY

Lay your sleeping head, my love,
Human on my faithless arm;
Time and fevers burn away
Individual beauty from
Thoughtful children, and the grave
Proves the child ephemeral:
But in my arms till break of day
Let the living creature lie,
Mortal, guilty, but to me
The entirely beautiful.

Soul and body have no bounds:
To lovers as they lie upon
Her tolerant enchanted slope
In their ordinary swoon,
Grave the vision Venus sends
Of supernatural sympathy,
Universal love and hope;
While an abstract insight wakes
Among the glaciers and the rocks
The hermit's carnal ecstasy.

Certainty, fidelity
On the stroke of midnight pass
Like vibrations of a bell
And fashionable madmen raise
Their pedantic boring cry:
Every farthing of the cost,
All the dreaded cards foretell,
Shall be paid, but from this night
Not a whisper, not a thought,
Not a kiss nor look be lost.

Beauty, midnight, vision dies:
Let the winds of dawn that blow
Softly round your dreaming head
Such a day of welcome show
Eye and knocking heart may bless,
Find our mortal world enough;
Noons of dryness find you fed
By the involuntary powers,
Nights of insult let you pass
Watched by every human love.

AS HE IS

Wrapped in a yielding air, beside
   The flower's noiseless hunger,
Close to the tree's clandestine tide,
   Close to the bird's high fever,
   Loud in his hope and anger,
Erect about a skeleton,
   Stands the expressive lover,
   Stands the deliberate man.

Beneath the hot unasking sun,
   Past stronger beasts and fairer
He picks his way, a living gun,
   With gun and lens and bible,
   A militant enquirer,
The friend, the rash, the enemy,
   The essayist, the able,
   Able at times to cry.

The friendless and unhated stone
   Lies everywhere about him,
The Brothered-One, the Not-Alone,
   The brothered and the hated

Whose family have taught him
To set against the large and dumb,
    The timeless and the rooted,
    His money and his time.

For mother's fading hopes become
    Dull wives to his dull spirits,
Soon dulled by nurse's moral thumb,
    That dullard fond betrayer,
    And, childish, he inherits,
So soon by legal father tricked,
    The tall imposing tower,
    Imposing, yes, but locked.

And ruled by dead men never met,
    By pious guess deluded,
Upon the stool of mania set
    Or stool of desolation,
    Sits murderous and clear-headed;
Enormous beauties round him move,
    For grandiose is his vision
    And grandiose his love.

Determined on Time's truthful shield
    The lamb must face the tigress,
Their faithful quarrel never healed
    Though, faithless, he consider
    His dream of vaguer ages,
Hunter and victim reconciled,
    The lion and the adder,
    The adder and the child.

Fresh loves betray him, every day
    Over his green horizon
A fresh deserter rides away,
    And miles away birds mutter
    Of ambush and of treason;
To fresh defeats he still must move,
    To further griefs and greater,
    And the defeat of grief.

THE CAPITAL

Quarter of pleasures where the rich are always waiting,
Waiting expensively for miracles to happen,
Dim-lighted restaurant where lovers eat each other,
Café where exiles have established a malicious village:

You with your charm and your apparatus have abolished
The strictness of winter and the spring's compulsion;
Far from your lights the outraged punitive father,
The dullness of mere obedience here is apparent.

So with orchestras and glances, soon you betray us
To belief in our infinite powers; and the innocent
Unobservant offender falls in a moment
Victim to his heart's invisible furies.

In unlighted streets you hide away the appalling;
Factories where lives are made for a temporary use
Like collars or chairs, rooms where the
                                        lonely are battered
Slowly like pebbles into fortuitous shapes.

But the sky you illumine, your glow is visible far
Into the dark countryside, enormous and frozen,
Where, hinting at the forbidden like a wicked uncle,
Night after night to the farmer's children you beckon.

MUSÉE DES BEAUX ARTS

About suffering they were never wrong,
The Old Masters: how well they understood
Its human position; how it takes place
While someone else is eating or opening a window or
                                  just walking dully along;
How, when the aged are reverently, passionately waiting
For the miraculous birth, there always must be
Children who did not specially want it to happen, skating
On a pond at the edge of the wood:
They never forgot
That even the dreadful martyrdom must run its course
Anyhow in a corner, some untidy spot
Where the dogs go on with their doggy life and the
                                  torturer's horse
Scratches its innocent behind on a tree.

In Brueghel's *Icarus*, for instance: how everything
                                  turns away
Quite leisurely from the disaster; the ploughman may
Have heard the splash, the forsaken cry,
But for him it was not an important failure; the sun shone
As it had to on the white legs disappearing into the green
Water; and the expensive delicate ship that must have seen
Something amazing, a boy falling out of the sky,
Had somewhere to get to and sailed calmly on.

THE NOVELIST

Encased in talent like a uniform,
The rank of every poet is well known;
They can amaze us like a thunderstorm,
Or die so young, or live for years alone.

They can dash forward like hussars: but he
Must struggle out of his boyish gift and learn
How to be plain and awkward, how to be
One after whom none think it worth to turn.

For, to achieve his lightest wish, he must
Become the whole of boredom, subject to
Vulgar complaints like love, among the Just

Be just, among the Filthy filthy too,
And in his own weak person, if he can,
Dully put up with all the wrongs of Man.

THE COMPOSER

All the others translate: the painter sketches
A visible world to love or reject;
Rummaging into his living, the poet fetches
The images out that hurt and connect,

From Life to Art by painstaking adaption,
Relying on us to cover the rift;
Only your notes are pure contraption,
Only your song is an absolute gift.

Pour out your presence, a delight cascading
The falls of the knee and the weirs of the spine,
Our climate of silence and doubt invading;

You alone, alone, imaginary song,
Are unable to say an existence is wrong,
And pour out your forgiveness like a wine.

EPITAPH ON A TYRANT

Perfection, of a kind, was what he was after,
And the poetry he invented was easy to understand;
He knew human folly like the back of his hand,
And was greatly interested in armies and fleets;
When he laughed, respectable senators burst
                                with laughter,
And when he cried the little children died in the streets.

IN MEMORY OF W. B. YEATS
(d. Jan. 1939)

I

He disappeared in the dead of winter:
The brooks were frozen, the airports almost deserted,
And snow disfigured the public statues;
The mercury sank in the mouth of the dying day.
What instruments we have agree
The day of his death was a dark cold day.

Far from his illness
The wolves ran on through the evergreen forests,
The peasant river
                was untempted by the fashionable quays;
By mourning tongues
The death of the poet was kept from his poems.

But for him it was his last afternoon as himself,
An afternoon of nurses and rumours;
The provinces of his body revolted,
The squares of his mind were empty,
Silence invaded the suburbs,
The current of his feeling failed; he became
                      his admirers.

Now he is scattered among a hundred cities
And wholly given over to unfamiliar affections,
To find his happiness in another kind of wood
And be punished under a foreign code of conscience.
The words of a dead man
Are modified in the guts of the living.

But in the importance and noise of to-morrow
When the brokers are roaring like beasts on the floor
                                        of the Bourse,
And the poor have the sufferings to which they are
                                        fairly accustomed,
And each in the cell of himself is almost
                                        convinced of his freedom,
A few thousand will think of this day
As one thinks of a day when one did something
                                        slightly unusual.

What instruments we have agree
The day of his death was a dark cold day.

II

You were silly like us; your gift survived it all:
The parish of rich women, physical decay,
Yourself. Mad Ireland hurt you into poetry.
Now Ireland has her madness and her weather still,
For poetry makes nothing happen: it survives
In the valley of its making where executives
Would never want to tamper, flows on south
From ranches of isolation and the busy griefs,
Raw towns that we believe and die in; it survives,
A way of happening, a mouth.

III

Earth, receive an honoured guest:
William Yeats is laid to rest.
Let the Irish vessel lie
Emptied of its poetry.

In the nightmare of the dark
All the dogs of Europe bark,
And the living nations wait,
Each sequestered in its hate;

Intellectual disgrace
Stares from every human face,
And the seas of pity lie
Locked and frozen in each eye.

Follow, poet, follow right
To the bottom of the night,
With your unconstraining voice
Still persuade us to rejoice;

With the farming of a verse
Make a vineyard of the curse,
Sing of human unsuccess
In a rapture of distress;

In the deserts of the heart
Let the healing fountain start,
In the prison of his days
Teach the free man how to praise.

THE UNKNOWN CITIZEN

(To JS/07/M/378
This Marble Monument Is Erected by the State)

He was found by the Bureau of Statistics to be
One against whom there was no official complaint,
And all the reports on his conduct agree
That, in the modern sense of an old-fashioned word,
                              he was a saint,
For in everything he did he served the Greater
                              Community.
Except for the War till the day he retired
He worked in a factory and never got fired,
But satisfied his employers, Fudge Motors Inc.
Yet he wasn't a scab or odd in his views,
For his Union reports that he paid his dues,
(Our report on his Union shows it was sound)
And our Social Psychology workers found
That he was popular with his mates and liked a drink.
The Press are convinced that he bought a paper
                              every day
And that his reactions to advertisements were normal
                              in every way.
Policies taken out in his name prove that he was fully
                              insured,

And his Health-card shows he was once in hospital but
                                                    left it cured.
Both Producers Research and High-Grade Living
                                                    declare
He was fully sensible to the advantages of the
                                                    Instalment Plan
And had everything necessary to the Modern Man,
A phonograph, a radio, a car and a frigidaire.
Our researchers into Public Opinion are content
That he held the proper opinions for the time of year;
When there was peace, he was for peace; when there
                                                    was war, he went.
He was married and added five children to the
                                                    population,
Which our Eugenist says was the right number for a
                                                    parent of his generation,
And our teachers report that he never interfered with
                                                    their education.
Was he free? Was he happy? The question is absurd:
Had anything been wrong, we should certainly
                                                    have heard.

THE PROPHETS

Perhaps I always knew what they were saying:
Even those earliest messengers who walked
Into my life from books where they were staying,
Those beautiful machines that never talked
But let the small boy worship them and learn
All their long names whose hardness made him proud;
Love was the word they never said aloud
As nothing that a picture can return.

And later when I hunted the Good Place,
Abandoned lead-mines let themselves be caught;
There was no pity in the adit's face,
The rusty winding-engine never taught
One obviously too apt, to say Too Late:
Their lack of shyness was a way of praising
Just what I didn't know, why I was gazing,
While all their lack of answer whispered 'Wait,'
And taught me gradually without coercion,
And all the landscape round them pointed to
The calm with which they took complete desertion
As proof that you existed.

It was true.
For now I have the answer from the face
That never will go back into a book
But asks for all my life, and is the Place
Where all I touch is moved to an embrace,
And there is no such thing as a vain look.

THE RIDDLE

Underneath the leaves of life,
Green on the prodigious tree,
   In a trance of grief
Stand the fallen man and wife:
Far away a single stag
Banished to a lonely crag
Gazes placid out to sea,
While from thickets round about
Breeding animals look in
   On Duality,
And small birds fly in and out
   Of the world of man.

Down in order from a ridge,
Bayonets glittering in the sun,
   Soldiers who will judge
Wind towards a little bridge:
Even orators may speak
Truths of value to the weak,
Necessary acts are done
By the ill and the unjust;
But the Judgement and the Smile,
   Though these two-in-one
See creation as they must,
   None shall reconcile.

Bordering our middle earth
Kingdoms of the Short and Tall,
    Rivals for our faith,
Stir up envy from our birth:
So the giant who storms the sky
In an angry wish to die
Wakes the hero in us all,
While the tiny with their power
To divide and hide and flee,
    When our fortunes fall,
Tempt to a belief in our
    Immortality.

Lovers running each to each
Feel such timid dreams catch fire
    Blazing as they touch,
Learn what love alone can teach:
Happy on a tousled bed
Praise Blake's acumen who said:
'One thing only we require
Of each other; we must see
In another's lineaments
    Gratified desire';
That is our humanity;
    Nothing else contents.

Nowhere else could I have known
Than, beloved, in your eyes
    What we have to learn,
That we love ourselves alone:
All our terrors burned away
We can learn at last to say:
'All our knowledge comes to this,
That existence is enough,
That in savage solitude
    Or the play of love
Every living creature is
    Woman, Man, and Child'.

LAW LIKE LOVE

Law, say the gardeners, is the sun,
Law is the one
All gardeners obey
To-morrow, yesterday, to-day.

Law is the wisdom of the old,
The impotent grandfathers feebly scold;
The grandchildren put out a treble tongue,
Law is the senses of the young.

Law, says the priest with a priestly look,
Expounding to an unpriestly people,
Law is the words in my priestly book,
Law is my pulpit and my steeple.
Law, says the judge as he looks down his nose,
Speaking clearly and most severely,
Law is as I've told you before,
Law is as you know I suppose,
Law is but let me explain it once more,
Law is The Law.

Yet law-abiding scholars write:
Law is neither wrong nor right,
Law is only crimes
Punished by places and by times,

Law is the clothes men wear
Anytime, anywhere,
Law is Good-morning and Good-night.

Others say, Law is our Fate;
Others say, Law is our State;
Others say, others say
Law is no more,
Law has gone away.

And always the loud angry crowd,
Very angry and very loud,
Law is We,
And always the soft idiot softly Me.

If we, dear, know we know no more
Than they about the Law,
If I no more than you
Know what we should and should not do
Except that all agree
Gladly or miserably
That the Law is
And that all know this,
If therefore thinking it absurd
To identify Law with some other word,
Unlike so many men
I cannot say Law is again,

No more than they can we suppress
The universal wish to guess
Or slip out of our own position
Into an unconcerned condition.

Although I can at least confine
Your vanity and mine
To stating timidly
A timid similarity,
We shall boast anyway:
Like love I say.

Like love we don't know where or why,
Like love we can't compel or fly,
Like love we often weep,
Like love we seldom keep.

THE HIDDEN LAW

The Hidden Law does not deny
Our laws of probability,
But takes the atom and the star
And human beings as they are,
And answers nothing when we lie.

It is the only reason why
No government can codify,
And verbal definitions mar
      The Hidden Law.

Its utter patience will not try
To stop us if we want to die:
When we escape It in a car,
When we forget It in a bar,
These are the ways we're punished by
      The Hidden Law.

REFUGEE BLUES

Say this city has ten million souls,
Some are living in mansions, some are living in holes:
Yet there's no place for us, my dear, yet there's
                         no place for us.

Once we had a country and we thought it fair,
Look in the atlas and you'll find it there:
We cannot go there now, my dear, we cannot go there
                                 now.

In the village churchyard there grows an old yew,
Every spring it blossoms anew:
Old passports can't do that, my dear, old passports
                            can't do that.

The consul banged the table and said:
'If you've got no passport you're officially dead':
But we are still alive, my dear, but we are still alive.

Went to a committee; they offered me a chair;
Asked me politely to return next year:
But where shall we go to-day, my dear, but where shall
                           we go to-day?

Came to a public meeting; the speaker got up and said:
'If we let them in, they will steal our daily bread';
He was talking of you and me, my dear, he was talking
of you and me.

Thought I heard the thunder rumbling in the sky;
It was Hitler over Europe, saying: 'They must die';
We were in his mind, my dear, we were in his mind.

Saw a poodle in a jacket fastened with a pin,
Saw a door opened and a cat let in:
But they weren't German Jews, my dear, but they
weren't German Jews.

Went down to the harbour and stood upon the quay,
Saw the fish swimming as if they were free:
Only ten feet away, my dear, only ten feet away.

Walked through a wood, saw the birds in the trees;
They had no politicians and sang at their ease:
They weren't the human race, my dear, they weren't
the human race.

Dreamed I saw a building with a thousand floors,
A thousand windows and a thousand doors;
Not one of them was ours, my dear, not one of them
         was ours.

Stood on a great plain in the falling snow;
Ten thousand soldiers marched to and fro:
Looking for you and me, my dear, looking for you
         and me.

CALYPSO

Driver drive faster and make a good run
Down the Springfield Line under the shining sun.

Fly like an aeroplane, don't pull up short
Till you brake for Grand Central Station, New York.

For there in the middle of that waiting-hall
Should be standing the one that I love best of all.

If he's not there to meet me when I get to town,
I'll stand on the side-walk with tears rolling down.

For he is the one that I love to look on,
The acme of kindness and perfection.

He presses my hand and he says he loves me,
Which I find an admirable peculiarity.

The woods are bright green on both sides of the line;
The trees have their loves though they're different
                                                    from mine.

But the poor fat old banker in the sun-parlor car
Has no one to love him except his cigar.

If Í were the Head of the Church or the State,
I'd powder my nose and just tell them to wait.

For love's more important and powerful than
Éven a priest or a politician.

EYES LOOK INTO THE WELL

Eyes look into the well,
Tears run down from the eye;
The tower cracked and fell
From the quiet winter sky.

Under a midnight stone
Love was buried by thieves;
The robbed heart begs for a bone,
The damned rustle like leaves.

Face down in the flooded brook
With nothing more to say,
Lies One the soldiers took,
And spoiled and threw away.

DOMESDAY SONG

Jumbled in one common box
Of their dark stupidity,
Orchid, swan, and Caesar lie;
Time that tires of everyone
Has corroded all the locks,
Thrown away the key for fun.

In its cleft a torrent mocks
Prophets who in days gone by
Made a profit on each cry,
Persona grata now with none;
And a jackass language shocks
Poets who can only pun.

Silence settles on the clocks;
Nursing mothers point a sly
Index finger at a sky,
Crimson in the setting sun;
In the valley of the fox
Gleams the barrel of a gun.

Once we could have made the docks,
Now it is too late to fly;
Once too often you and I
Did what we should not have done;
Round the rampant rugged rocks
Rude and ragged rascals run.

IN MEMORY OF SIGMUND FREUD
(d. Sept. 1939)

When there are so many we shall have to mourn,
when grief has been made so public, and exposed
    to the critique of a whole epoch
   the frailty of our conscience and anguish,

of whom shall we speak? For every day they die
among us, those who were doing us some good,
    who knew it was never enough but
   hoped to improve a little by living.

Such was this doctor: still at eighty he wished
to think of our life from whose unruliness
    so many plausible young futures
   with threats or flattery ask obedience,

but his wish was denied him: he closed his eyes
upon that last picture, common to us all,
    of problems like relatives gathered
   puzzled and jealous about our dying.

For about him till the very end were still
those he had studied, the fauna of the night,
    and shades that still waited to enter
   the bright circle of his recognition

turned elsewhere with their disappointment as he
was taken away from his life interest
    to go back to the earth in London,
  an important Jew who died in exile.

Only Hate was happy, hoping to augment
his practice now, and his dingy clientele
    who think they can be cured by killing
  and covering the gardens with ashes.

They are still alive, but in a world he changed
simply by looking back with no false regrets;
    all he did was to remember
  like the old and be honest like children.

He wasn't clever at all: he merely told
the unhappy Present to recite the Past
    like a poetry lesson till sooner
  or later it faltered at the line where

long ago the accusations had begun,
and suddenly knew by whom it had been judged,
    how rich life had been and how silly,
  and was life-forgiven and more humble,

able to approach the Future as a friend
without a wardrobe of excuses, without
    a set mask of rectitude or an
  embarrassing over-familiar gesture.

No wonder the ancient cultures of conceit
in his technique of unsettlement foresaw
    the fall of princes, the collapse of
  their lucrative patterns of frustration:

if he succeeded, why, the Generalised Life
would become impossible, the monolith
    of State be broken and prevented
  the co-operation of avengers.

Of course they called on God, but he went his way
down among the lost people like Dante, down
    to the stinking fosse where the injured
  lead the ugly life of the rejected,

and showed us what evil is, not, as we thought,
deeds that must be punished, but our lack of faith,
    our dishonest mood of denial,
  the concupiscence of the oppressor.

If some traces of the autocratic pose,
the paternal strictness he distrusted, still
    clung to his utterance and features,
   it was a protective coloration

for one who'd lived among enemies so long:
if often he was wrong and, at times, absurd,
    to us he is no more a person
   now but a whole climate of opinion

under whom we conduct our different lives:
Like weather he can only hinder or help,
    the proud can still be proud but find it
   a little harder, the tyrant tries to

make do with him but doesn't care for him much:
he quietly surrounds all our habits of growth
    and extends, till the tired in even
   the remotest miserable duchy

have felt the change in their bones and are cheered,
till the child, unlucky in his little State,
    some hearth where freedom is excluded,
   a hive whose honey is fear and worry,

feels calmer now and somehow assured of escape,
while, as they lie in the grass of our neglect,
    so many long-forgotten objects
    revealed by his undiscouraged shining

are returned to us and made precious again;
games we had thought we must drop as we grew up,
    little noises we dared not laugh at,
    faces we made when no one was looking.

But he wishes us more than this. To be free
is often to be lonely. He would unite
    the unequal moieties fractured
    by our own well-meaning sense of justice,

would restore to the larger the wit and will
the smaller possesses but can only use
    for arid disputes, would give back to
    the son the mother's richness of feeling:

but he would have us remember most of all
to be enthusiastic over the night,
    not only for the sense of wonder
    it alone has to offer, but also

because it needs our love. With large sad eyes
its delectable creatures look up and beg
        us dumbly to ask them to follow:
    they are exiles who long for the future

that lies in our power, they too would rejoice
if allowed to serve enlightenment like him,
        even to bear our cry of 'Judas',
    as he did and all must bear who serve it.

One rational voice is dumb. Over his grave
the household of Impulse mourns one dearly loved:
        sad is Eros, builder of cities,
    and weeping anarchic Aphrodite.

HELL

Hell is neither here nor there,
Hell is not anywhere,
Hell is hard to bear.

It is so hard to dream posterity
Or haunt a ruined century
And so much easier to be.

Only the challenge to our will,
Our pride in learning any skill,
Sustains our effort to be ill.

To talk the dictionary through
Without a chance word coming true
Is more than Darwin's apes could do.

Yet pride alone could not insist
Did we not hope, if we persist,
That one day Hell might actually exist.

In time, pretending to be blind
And universally unkind
Might really send us out of our mind.

If we were really wretched and asleep
It would be then *de trop* to weep,
It would be natural to lie,
There'd be no living left to die.

LADY WEEPING AT THE CROSSROADS

Lady, weeping at the crossroads,
Would you meet your love
In the twilight with his greyhounds,
And the hawk on his glove?

Bribe the birds then on the branches,
Bribe them to be dumb,
Stare the hot sun out of heaven
That the night may come.

Starless are the nights of travel,
Bleak the winter wind;
Run with terror all before you
And regret behind.

Run until you hear the ocean's
Everlasting cry;
Deep though it may be and bitter
You must drink it dry,

Wear out patience in the lowest
Dungeons of the sea,
Searching through the stranded shipwrecks
For the golden key,

Push on to the world's end, pay the
Dread guard with a kiss,
Cross the rotten bridge that totters
Over the abyss.

There stands the deserted castle
Ready to explore;
Enter, climb the marble staircase,
Open the locked door.

Cross the silent empty ballroom,
Doubt and danger past;
Blow the cobwebs from the mirror,
See yourself at last.

Put your hand behind the wainscot,
You have done your part;
Find the penknife there and plunge it
Into your false heart.

DIASPORA

How he survived them they could never understand:
Had they not beggared him themselves to prove
They could not live without their dogmas or their land?

No worlds they drove him from were ever big enough:
How *could* it be the earth the Unconfined
Meant when It bade them set no limits to their love?

And he fulfilled the rôle for which he was designed:
On heat with fear, he drew their terrors to him,
And was a godsend to the lowest of mankind,

Till there was no place left where they could still
                                        pursue him
Except that exile which he called his race.
But, envying him even that, they plunged right
                                        through him

Into a land of mirrors without time or space,
And all they had to strike now was the human face.

BLESSED EVENT

Round the three actors in any blessed event
Is always standing an invisible audience of four,
The double twins, the fallen natures of man.

On the Left they remember difficult childhoods,
On the Right they have forgotten
                                    why they were so happy,
Above sit the best decisive people,
Below they must kneel all day so as not to be governed.

Four voices just audible in the hush of any Christmas:
Accept my friendship or die.
I shall keep order and not very much will happen.
Bring me luck and of course I'll support you.
I smell blood and an era of prominent madmen.

But the Three hear nothing and are blind even to
                                         the landscape
With its towns and rivers and pretty pieces of nonsense.

He, all father, repenting their animal nights,
Cries: *Why did She have to be tortured? It is all my fault.*
Once more a virgin, She whispers: *The Future shall
never suffer.*
And the New Life awkwardly touches its home,
beginning to fumble
About in the Truth for the straight successful Way
Which will always appear to end in some dreadful defeat.

ALONE

Each lover has a theory of his own
About the difference between the ache
Of being with his love, and being alone:

Why what, when dreaming, is dear flesh and bone
That really stirs the senses, when awake,
Appears a simulacrum of his own.

Narcissus disbelieves in the unknown;
He cannot join his image in the lake
So long as he assumes he is alone.

The child, the waterfall, the fire, the stone,
Are always up to mischief, though, and take
The universe for granted as their own.

The elderly, like Proust, are always prone
To think of love as a subjective fake;
The more they love, the more they feel alone.

Whatever view we hold, it must be shown
Why every lover has a wish to make
Some other kind of otherness his own:
Perhaps, in fact, we never are alone.

LEAP BEFORE YOU LOOK

The sense of danger must not disappear:
The way is certainly both short and steep,
However gradual it looks from here;
Look if you like, but you will have to leap.

Tough-minded men get mushy in their sleep
And break the by-laws any fool can keep;
It is not the convention but the fear
That has a tendency to disappear.

The worried efforts of the busy heap,
The dirt, the imprecision, and the beer
Produce a few smart wisecracks every year;
Laugh if you can, but you will have to leap.

The clothes that are considered right to wear
Will not be either sensible or cheap,
So long as we consent to live like sheep
And never mention those who disappear.

Much can be said for social savoir-faire,
But to rejoice when no one else is there
Is even harder than it is to weep;
No one is watching, but you have to leap.

A solitude ten thousand fathoms deep
Sustains the bed on which we lie, my dear:
Although I love you, you will have to leap;
Our dream of safety has to disappear.

IF I COULD TELL YOU

Time will say nothing but I told you so,
Time only knows the price we have to pay;
If I could tell you I would let you know.

If we should weep when clowns put on their show,
If we should stumble when musicians play,
Time will say nothing but I told you so.

There are no fortunes to be told, although,
Because I love you more than I can say,
If I could tell you I would let you know.

The winds must come from somewhere when they blow,
There must be reasons why the leaves decay;
Time will say nothing but I told you so.

Perhaps the roses really want to grow,
The vision seriously intends to stay;
If I could tell you I would let you know.

Suppose the lions all get up and go,
And all the brooks and soldiers run away;
Will Time say nothing but I told you so?
If I could tell you I would let you know.

MANY HAPPY RETURNS
(for John Rettger)

Johnny, since to-day is
February the twelfth when
Neighbours and relations
    Think of you and wish,
Though a staunch Aquarian,
Graciously accept the
Verbal celebrations
    Of a doubtful Fish.

Seven years ago you
Warmed your mother's heart by
Making a successful
    Début on our stage;
Naïveté's an act that
You already know you
Cannot get away with
    Even at your age.

So I wish you first a
Sense of theatre; only
Those who love illusion
    And know it will go far:
Otherwise we spend our
Lives in a confusion
Of what we say and do with
    Who we really are.

You will any day now
Have this revelation:
'Why, we're all like people
    Acting in a play.'
And will suffer, Johnny,
Man's unique temptation
Precisely at the moment
    You utter this cliché.

Remember if you can then,
Only the All-Father
Can change the cast or give them
    Easier lines to say;
Deliberate interference
With others for their own good
Is not allowed the author
    Of the play within The Play.

Just because our pride's an
Evil there's no end to,
Birthdays and the arts are
     Justified, for when
We consciously pretend to
Own the earth or play at
Being gods, thereby we
     Own that we are men.

As a human creature
You will all too often
Forget your proper station,
     Johnny, like us all;
Therefore let your birthday
Be a wild occasion
Like a Saturnalia
     Or a Servants' Ball.

What else shall I wish you?
Following convention
Shall I wish you Beauty,
     Money, Happiness?
Or anything you mention?
No, for I recall an
Ancient proverb: – Nothing
     Fails like a success.

What limping devil sets our
Head and heart at variance,
That each time the Younger
    Generation sails,
The old and weather-beaten
Deny their own experience
And pray the gods to send them
    Calm seas, auspicious gales?

I'm not such an idiot
As to claim the power
To peer into the vistas
    Of your future, still
I'm prepared to guess you
Have not found your life as
Easy as your sister's
    And you never will.

If I'm right about this,
May you in your troubles,
Neither (like so many
    In the U.S.A.)
Be ashamed of any
Suffering as vulgar,
Nor bear them like a hero
    In the biggest way.

All the possibilities
It had to reject are
What give life and warmth to
    An actual character;
The roots of wit and charm tap
Secret springs of sorrow,
Every brilliant doctor
    Hides a murderer.

Then, since all self-knowledge
Tempts man into envy,
May you, by acquiring
    Proficiency in what
Whitehead calls the art of
Negative Prehension,
Love without desiring
    All that you are not.

Tao is a tightrope,
So to keep your balance,
May you always, Johnny,
    Manage to combine
Intellectual talents
With a sensual gusto,
The Socratic Doubt with
    The Socratic Sign.

That is all that I can
Think of at this moment
And it's time I brought these
    Verses to a close:
Happy Birthday, Johnny,
Live beyond your income,
Travel for enjoyment,
    Follow your own nose.

THE LESSON

The first time that I dreamed, we were in flight,
And fagged with running; there was civil war,
A valley full of thieves and wounded bears.

Farms blazed behind us; turning to the right,
We came at once to a tall house, its door
Wide open, waiting for its long-lost heirs.

An elderly clerk sat on the bedroom stairs
Writing; but we had tiptoed past him when
He raised his head and stuttered – 'Go away'.

We wept and begged to stay:
He wiped his pince-nez, hesitated, then
Said no, he had no power to give us leave;
Our lives were not in order; we must leave.

*   *   *

The second dream began in a May wood;
We had been laughing; your blue eyes were kind,
Your excellent nakedness without disdain.

Our lips met, wishing universal good;
But, on their impact, sudden flame and wind
Fetched you away and turned me loose again

122

To make a focus for a wide wild plain,
Dead level and dead silent and bone dry,
Where nothing could have suffered, sinned, or grown.
On a high chair alone
I sat, a little master, asking why
The cold and solid object in my hands
Should be a human hand, one of your hands.

*   *   *

And the last dream was this: we were to go
To a great banquet and a Victory Ball
After some tournament or dangerous test.

Our cushions were of crimson velvet, so
We must have won; though there were crowns for all,
Ours were of gold, of paper all the rest.

Fair, wise or funny was each famous guest,
Love smiled at Courage over priceless glass,
And rockets died in hundreds to express
Our learned carelessness.
A band struck up; all over the green grass
A sea of paper crowns rose up to dance:
Ours were too heavy; we did not dance.

*   *   *

I woke. You were not there. But as I dressed
Anxiety turned to shame, feeling all three
Intended one rebuke. For had not each
In its own way tried to teach
My will to love you that it cannot be,
As I think, of such consequence to want
What anyone is given, if they want?

THE FALL OF ROME
(*for Cyril Connolly*)

The piers are pummelled by the waves;
In a lonely field the rain
Lashes an abandoned train;
Outlaws fill the mountain caves.

Fantastic grow the evening gowns;
Agents of the Fisc pursue
Absconding tax-defaulters through
The sewers of provincial towns.

Private rites of magic send
The temple prostitutes to sleep;
All the literati keep
An imaginary friend.

Cerebrotonic Cato may
Extol the Ancient Disciplines,
But the muscle-bound Marines
Mutiny for food and pay.

Caesar's double-bed is warm
As an unimportant clerk
Writes *I DO NOT LIKE MY WORK*
On a pink official form.

Unendowed with wealth or pity,
Little birds with scarlet legs,
Sitting on their speckled eggs,
Eye each flu-infected city.

Altogether elsewhere, vast
Herds of reindeer move across
Miles and miles of golden moss,
Silently and very fast.

A WALK AFTER DARK

A cloudless night like this
Can set the spirit soaring:
After a tiring day
The clockwork spectacle is
Impressive in a slightly boring
Eighteenth-century way.

It soothed adolescence a lot
To meet so shameless a stare;
The things I did could not
Be so shocking as they said
If that would still be there
After the shocked were dead.

Now, unready to die
But already at the stage
When one starts to resent the young,
I am glad those points in the sky
May also be counted among
The creatures of middle-age.

It's cosier thinking of night
As more an Old People's Home
Than a shed for a faultless machine,
That the red pre-Cambrian light
Is gone like Imperial Rome
Or myself at seventeen.

Yet however much we may like
The stoic manner in which
The classical authors wrote,
Only the young and the rich
Have the nerve or the figure to strike
The lacrimae rerum note.

For the present stalks abroad
Like the past and its wronged again
Whimper and are ignored,
And the truth cannot be hid;
Somebody chose their pain,
What needn't have happened did.

Occurring this very night
By no established rule,
Some event may already have hurled
Its first little No at the right
Of the laws we accept to school
Our post-diluvian world:

But the stars burn on overhead,
Unconscious of final ends,
As I walk home to bed,
Asking what judgement waits
My person, all my friends,
And these United States.

ALONSO TO FERDINAND

Dear Son, when the warm multitudes cry,
Ascend your throne majestically,
But keep in mind the waters where fish
See sceptres descending with no wish
To touch them; sit regal and erect,
But imagine the sands where a crown
Has the status of a broken-down
Sofa or mutilated statue:
Remember as bells and cannon boom
The cold deep that does not envy you,
The sunburnt superficial kingdom
Where a king is an object.

Expect no help from others, for who
Talk sense to princes or refer to
The scorpion in official speeches
As they unveil some granite Progress
Leading a child and holding a bunch
Of lilies? In their Royal Zoos the
Shark and the octopus are tactfully
Omitted; synchronised clocks march on
Within their powers: without, remain
The ocean flats where no subscription
Concerts are given, the desert plain
Where there is nothing for lunch.

Only your darkness can tell you what
A prince's ornate mirror dare not,
Which you should fear more – the sea in which
A tyrant sinks entangled in rich
Robes while a mistress turns a white back
Upon his splutter, or the desert
Where an emperor stands in his shirt
While his diary is read by sneering
Beggars, and far off he notices
A lean horror flapping and hopping
Toward him with inhuman swiftness:
Learn from your dreams what you lack,

For as your fears are, so must you hope.
The Way of Justice is a tightrope
Where no prince is safe for one instant
Unless he trust his embarrassment,
As in his left ear the siren sings
Meltingly of water and a night
Where all flesh had peace, and on his right
The efreet offers a brilliant void
Where his mind could be perfectly clear
And all his limitations destroyed:
Many young princes soon disappear
To join all the unjust kings.

So, if you prosper, suspect those bright
Mornings when you whistle with a light
Heart. You are loved; you have never seen
The harbour so still, the park so green,
So many well-fed pigeons upon
Cupolas and triumphal arches,
So many stags and slender ladies
Beside the canals. Remember when
Your climate seems a permanent home
For marvellous creatures and great men,
What griefs and convulsions startled Rome,
Ecbatana, Babylon.

How narrow the space, how slight the chance
For civil pattern and importance
Between the watery vagueness and
The triviality of the sand,
How soon the lively trip is over
From loose craving to sharp aversion,
Aimless jelly to paralysed bone:
At the end of each successful day
Remember that the fire and the ice
Are never more than one step away
From the temperate city; it is
But a moment to either.

But should you fail to keep your kingdom
And, like your father before you, come
Where thought accuses and feeling mocks,
Believe your pain: praise the scorching rocks
For their desiccation of your lust,
Thank the bitter treatment of the tide
For its dissolution of your pride,
That the whirlwind may arrange your will
And the deluge release it to find
The spring in the desert, the fruitful
Island in the sea, where flesh and mind
Are delivered from mistrust.

Blue the sky beyond her humming sail
As I sit to-day by our ship's rail
Watching exuberant porpoises
Escort us homeward and writing this
For you to open when I am gone:
Read it, Ferdinand, with the blessing
Of Alonso, your father, once King
Of Naples, now ready to welcome
Death, but rejoicing in a new love,
A new peace, having heard the solemn
Music strike and seen the statue move
To forgive our illusion.

SONG OF THE MASTER AND BOATSWAIN

At Dirty Dick's and Sloppy Joe's
   We drank our liquor straight,
Some went upstairs with Margery,
   And some, alas, with Kate;
And two by two like cat and mouse
The homeless played at keeping house.

There Wealthy Meg, the Sailor's Friend,
   And Marion, cow-eyed,
Opened their arms to me but I
   Refused to step inside;
I was not looking for a cage
In which to mope in my old age.

The nightingales are sobbing in
   The orchards of our mothers,
And hearts that we broke long ago
   Have long been breaking others;
Tears are round, the sea is deep:
Roll them overboard and sleep.

MIRANDA'S SONG

My Dear One is mine as mirrors are lonely,
As the poor and sad are real to the good king,
And the high green hill sits always by the sea.

Up jumped the Black Man behind the elder tree,
Turned a somersault and ran away waving;
My Dear One is mine as mirrors are lonely.

The Witch gave a squawk; her venomous body
Melted into light as water leaves a spring,
And the high green hill sits always by the sea.

At his crossroads, too, the Ancient prayed for me;
Down his wasted cheeks tears of joy were running:
My Dear One is mine as mirrors are lonely.

He kissed me awake, and no one was sorry;
The sun shone on sails, eyes, pebbles, anything,
And the high green hill sits always by the sea.

So, to remember our changing garden, we
Are linked as children in a circle dancing:
My Dear One is mine as mirrors are lonely,
And the high green hill sits always by the sea.

IN PRAISE OF LIMESTONE

If it form the one landscape that we, the inconstant ones,
    Are consistently homesick for, this is chiefly
Because it dissolves in water. Mark these rounded slopes
    With their surface fragrance of thyme and, beneath,
A secret system of caves and conduits; hear the springs
    That spurt out everywhere with a chuckle,
Each filling a private pool for its fish and carving
    Its own little ravine whose cliffs entertain
The butterfly and the lizard; examine this region
    Of short distances and definite places:
What could be more like Mother or a fitter background
    For her son, the flirtatious male who lounges
Against a rock in the sunlight, never doubting
    That for all his faults he is loved; whose works are but
Extensions of his power to charm? From weathered
                                  outcrop
    To hill-top temple, from appearing waters to
Conspicuous fountains, from a wild to a formal
                                  vineyard,
    Are ingenious but short steps that a child's wish
To receive more attention than his brothers, whether

By pleasing or teasing, can easily take.
Watch, then, the band of rivals as they climb up and
                                    down
   Their steep stone gennels in twos and threes, at times
Arm in arm, but never, thank God, in step; or engaged
   On the shady side of a square at midday in
Voluble discourse, knowing each other too well to think
   There are any important secrets, unable
To conceive a god whose temper-tantrums are moral
   And not to be pacified by a clever line
Or a good lay: for, accustomed to a stone that responds,
   They have never had to veil their faces in awe
Of a crater whose blazing fury could not be fixed;
   Adjusted to the local needs of valleys
Where everything can be touched or reached by
                             walking,
   Their eyes have never looked into infinite space
Through the lattice-work of a nomad's comb;
                        born lucky,
   Their legs have never encountered the fungi
And insects of the jungle, the monstrous forms and lives
   With which we have nothing, we like to hope,
                      in common.

So, when one of them goes to the bad, the way his mind
                                                         works
    Remains comprehensible: to become a pimp
Or deal in fake jewellery or ruin a fine tenor voice
    For effects that bring down the
                                    house, could happen to all
But the best and the worst of us . . .
                                    That is why, I suppose,
    The best and worst never stayed here long
                                                but sought
Immoderate soils where the beauty was not so external,
    The light less public and the meaning of life
Something more than a mad camp. 'Come!' cried the
                                                granite wastes,
    'How evasive is your humor, how accidental
Your kindest kiss, how permanent is death.' (Saints-to-be
    Slipped away sighing.) 'Come!' purred the clays
                                                and gravels,
'On our plains there is room for armies to drill; rivers
    Wait to be tamed and slaves to construct you a tomb
In the grand manner: soft as the earth is mankind and
                                                        both
    Need to be altered.' (Intendant Caesars rose and
Left, slamming the door.) But the really reckless were
                                                        fetched

By an older colder voice, the oceanic whisper:
'I am the solitude that asks and promises nothing;
     That is how I shall set you free. There is no love;
There are only the various envies, all of them sad.'

     They were right, my dear, all those voices were right
And still are; this land is not the sweet home that
                                        it looks,
     Nor its peace the historical calm of a site
Where something was settled once and for all:
                                        A backward
     And dilapidated province, connected
To the big busy world by a tunnel, with a certain
     Seedy appeal, is that all it is now? Not quite:
It has a worldly duty which in spite of itself
     It does not neglect, but calls into question
All the Great Powers assume; it disturbs our rights.
                                        The poet,
     Admired for his earnest habit of calling
The sun the sun, his mind Puzzle, is made uneasy
     By these marble statues which so obviously doubt
His antimythological myth; and these gamins,
     Pursuing the scientist down the tiled colonnade
With such lively offers, rebuke his concern for Nature's
     Remotest aspects: I, too, am reproached, for what
And how much you know. Not to lose time, not to
                                        get caught,

Not to be left behind, not, please! to resemble
The beasts who repeat themselves, or a thing like water
    Or stone whose conduct can be predicted, these
Are our Common Prayer, whose greatest
                                    comfort is music
    Which can be made anywhere, is invisible,
And does not smell. In so far as we have to look forward
    To death as a fact, no doubt we are right: But if
Sins can be forgiven, if bodies rise from the dead,
    These modifications of matter into
Innocent athletes and gesticulating fountains,
    Made solely for pleasure, make a further point:
The blessed will not care what angle they are regarded
                                    from,
    Having nothing to hide. Dear, I know nothing of
Either, but when I try to imagine a faultless love
    Or the life to come, what I hear is the murmur
Of underground streams, what I see is a limestone
                                    landscape.

HUNTING SEASON

A shot: from crag to crag
   The tell-tale echoes trundle;
Some feathered he-or-she
   Is now a lifeless bundle
And, proud into a kitchen, some
Example of our tribe will come.

Down in the startled valley
   Two lovers break apart:
He hears the roaring oven
   Of a witch's heart;
Behind his murmurs of her name
She sees a marksman taking aim.

Reminded of the hour
   And that his chair is hard,
A deathless verse half done,
   One interrupted bard
Postpones his dying with a dish
Of several suffocated fish.

FLEET VISIT

The sailors come ashore
Out of their hollow ships,
Mild-looking middle-class boys
Who read the comic strips;
One baseball game is more
To them than fifty Troys.

They look a bit lost, set down
In this unamerican place
Where natives pass with laws
And futures of their own;
They are not here because
But only just-in-case.

The whore and ne'er-do-well
Who pester them with junk
In their grubby ways at least
Are serving the Social Beast;
They neither make nor sell –
No wonder they get drunk.

But their ships on the vehement blue
Of this harbor actually gain
From having nothing to do;
Without a human will
To tell them whom to kill
Their structures are humane

And, far from looking lost,
Look as if they were meant
To be pure abstract design
By some master of pattern and line,
Certainly worth every cent
Of the billions they must have cost.

ODE TO GAEA

From this new culture of the air we finally see,
far-shining in excellence, what our Mother, the
        nicest daughter of Chaos, would
     admire could she look in a glass,

and what, in her eyes, is natural: it is the old
grand style of gesture we watch as, heavy with cold,
        the top-waters of all her
     northern seas take their vernal plunge,

and suddenly her desolations, salt as blood,
prolix yet terse, are glamorously carpeted
        with great swatches of plankton,
     delicious spreads of nourishment,

while, in her realm of solids, lively dots expand,
companionship becomes an unstaid passion and
        leaves by the mile hide tons of
     pied pebbles that will soon be birds.

Now that we know how she looks, she
                              seems more mysterious
than when, in her *partibus infidelibus,*
        we painted sizzling dragons
     and wizards reading upside down,

but less approachable: where she joins girl's-ear lakes
to bird's-foot deltas with lead-blue squiggles she makes,
            surely, a value judgement,
        'of pure things Water is the best,'

but how does she rank wheelwrights? One doubts if
                                        she knows
which sub-species of folly is peculiar to those
            pretty molehills, where on that
        pocket-handkerchief of a plain

the syntax changes: peering down sleepily at
a crenellated shore, the tired old diplomat
            becomes embarrassed – Should he
        smile for 'our great good ally', scowl

at 'that vast and detestable empire' or choose
the sneer reserved for certain Southern countries 'whose
            status and moral climate
        we have no desire, sir, to emulate'?

But why we should feel neglected on mountain drives,
unpopular in woods, is quite clear; the older lives
            have no wish to be stood in
        rows or at right angles: below,

straight as its railroads, cutting diagonally across
a positivist republic, two lines of moss
   show where the Devil's Causeway
  drew pilgrims thirteen gods ago,

and on this eve of whispers and tapped telephones
before the Ninth Catastrophe, square corner-stones
   still distinguish a fortress
  of the High Kings from untutored rock.

Tempting to mortals is the fancy of half-concerned
Gods in the sky, of a bored Thunderer who turned
   from the Troy-centred grief to
  watch the Hippemolgoi drink their milk,

and how plausible from his look-point: we may well
shake a weak fist one day at this vision, but the spell
   of high places will haunt us
  long after our jaunt has declined,

as soon it must, to the hard ground. Where six foot is tall,
good-manners will ask easy riddles like 'Why are all
   the rowdiest marches and the
  most venomous iambics composed

by lame clergymen?', will tell no tales which end
                                        in worse
disaster than that of the tipsy poet who cursed
            a baby for whom later
        he came to sigh. So we were taught

before the Greater Engines came and the police
who go with them, when the long rivers
                                    ran through peace
            and the holy laws of Speech were
        held in awe, even by evil tongues,

and manners, maybe, will stand us in better stead,
down there, than a kantian conscience. From overhead
            much harm is discernible,
        farms unroofed and harbor-works wrecked

in the Second Assault; frank to an ungrieving sky
as still they look, too many fertilities lie
            in dread of the tormentor's
        fondling finger, and in the few

that still have poky shops and audiences of one,
many are overweight, the pious peasant's only son,
            goading their crumpled faces
        down innocence-corrupting roads,

dreams of cities where his cows are whores. When the wise
wilt in the glare of the Shadow, the stern advise
          tribute, and the large-hearted
     already talk Its gibberish,

perhaps a last stand in the passes will be made
by those whose Valhalla would be hearing verse by Praed
          or arias by Rossini
     between two entrées by Carême.

We hope so. But who on Cupid's Coming would care to bet?
More than one World's Bane has been
                              scotched before this, yet
          Justice during his *Te Deum*
     slipped away sighing from the hero's pew,

and Earth, till the end, will be Herself. She has never
                              been moved
except by Amphion, and orators have not improved
          since misled Athens perished
     upon Sicilian marble: what,

to Her, the real one, can our good landscapes be but lies,
those woods where tigers chum with
                              deer and no root dies,
          that tideless bay where children
     play Bishop on a golden shore?

WOODS
(*for Nicolas Nabokov*)

Sylvan meant savage in those primal woods
Piero di Cosimo so loved to draw,
Where nudes, bears, lions, sows with women's heads,
Mounted and murdered and ate each other raw,
Nor thought the lightning-kindled bush to tame
But, flabbergasted, fled the useful flame.

Reduced to patches, owned by hunting squires,
Of villages with ovens and a stocks,
They whispered still of most unsocial fires,
Though Crown and Mitre warned their silly flocks
The pasture's humdrum rhythms to approve
And to abhor the licence of the grove.

Guilty intention still looks for a hotel
That wants no details and surrenders none;
A wood is that, and throws in charm as well,
And many a semi-innocent, undone,
Has blamed its nightingales who round the deed
Sang with such sweetness of a happy greed.

Those birds, of course, did nothing of the sort,
And, as for sylvan nature, if you take
A snapshot at a picnic, O how short
And lower-ordersy the Gang will look
By those vast lives that never took another
And are not scared of gods, ghosts, or stepmother.

Among these coffins of its by-and-by
The Public can (it cannot on a coast)
Bridle its skirt-and-bargain-chasing eye,
And where should an austere philologist
Relax but in the very world of shade
From which the matter of his field was made.

Old sounds re-educate an ear grown coarse,
As Pan's green father suddenly raps out
A burst of indecipherable Morse,
And cuckoos mock in Welsh, and doves create
In rustic English over all they do
To rear their modern family of two.

Now here, now there, some loosened element,
A fruit in vigor or a dying leaf,
Utters its private idiom for descent,
And late man, listening through his latter grief,
Hears, close or far, the oldest of his joys,
Exactly as it was, the water noise.

A well-kempt forest begs Our Lady's grace;
Someone is not disgusted, or at least
Is laying bets upon the human race
Retaining enough decency to last;
The trees encountered on a country stroll
Reveal a lot about a country's soul.

A small grove massacred to the last ash,
An oak with heart-rot, give away the show:
This great society is going smash;
They cannot fool us with how fast they go,
How much they cost each other and the gods.
A culture is no better than its woods.

LAKES
(for Isaiah Berlin)

A lake allows an average father, walking slowly,
    To circumvent it in an afternoon,
And any healthy mother to halloo the children
    Back to her bedtime from their games across:
(Anything bigger than that, like Michigan or Baikal,
    Though potable, is an 'estranging sea').

Lake-folk require no fiend to keep them on their toes;
    They leave aggression to ill-bred romantics
Who duel with their shadows over blasted heaths:
    A month in a lacustrine atmosphere
Would find the fluvial rivals waltzing not exchanging
    The rhyming insults of their great-great-uncles.

No wonder Christendom did not get really started
    Till, scarred by torture, white from caves and jails,
Her pensive chiefs converged on the Ascanian Lake
    And by that stork-infested shore invented
The life of Godhead, making catholic the figure
    Of three small fishes in a triangle.

Sly Foreign Ministers should always meet beside one,
    For, whether they walk widdershins or deasil,
The path will yoke their shoulders to one liquid centre
    Like two old donkeys pumping as they plod;
Such physical compassion may not guarantee
    A marriage for their armies, but it helps.

Only a very wicked or conceited man,
    About to sink somewhere in mid-Atlantic,
Could think Poseidon's frown
                                was meant for him in person,
    But it is only human to believe
The little lady of the glacier lake has fallen
    In love with the rare bather whom she drowns.

The drinking water of the city where one panics
    At nothing noticing how real one is
May come from reservoirs whose guards are
                                all too conscious
    Of being followed: Webster's cardinal
Saw in a fish-pool something horrid with a hay-rake;
    I know a Sussex hammer-pond like that.

A haunted lake is sick, though; normally, they doctor
   Our tactile fevers with a visual world
Where beaks are dumb like boughs and faces calm
                                   like houses;
   The water-scorpion finds it quite unticklish,
And, if it shudder slightly when caressed by boats,
   It never asks for water or a loan.

Liking one's Nature, as lake-lovers do, benign
   Goes with a wish for savage dogs and man-traps:
One Fall, one dispossession, is enough, I'm sorry;
   Why should I give Lake Eden to the Nation
Just because every mortal Jack and Jill has been
   The genius of some amniotic mere?

It is unlikely I shall ever keep a swan
   Or build a tower on any small tombolo,
But that's not going to stop me wondering what sort
   Of lake I would decide on if I should.
Moraine, pot, oxbow, glint, sink, crater, piedmont,
                                   dimple ... ?
   Just reeling off their names is ever so comfy.

PLAINS
(for Wendell Johnson)

I can imagine quite easily ending up
    In a decaying port on a desolate coast,
Cadging drinks from the unwary, a quarrelsome,
    Disreputable old man; I can picture
A second childhood in a valley, scribbling
    Reams of edifying and unreadable verse;
But I cannot see a plain without a shudder:
    'Oh God, please, please, don't ever make me
                        live there!'

It's horrible to think what peaks come down to,
    That pecking rain and squelching glacier defeat
Tall pomps of stone where goddesses lay sleeping,
    Dreaming of being woken by some chisel's kiss,
That what those blind brutes leave when they are
                     through is nothing
    But a mere substance, a clay that meekly takes
The potter's cuff, a gravel that as concrete   ·
    Will unsex any space which it encloses.

And think of growing where all elsewheres are equal!
    So long as there's a hill-ridge somewhere the dreamer
Can place his land of marvels; in poor valleys

Orphans can head downstream to seek a million:
Here nothing points; to choose between Art and Science
An embryo genius would have to spin a stick.
What could these farms do if set loose but drift
like clouds,
What goal of unrest is there but the Navy?

Romance? Not in this weather. Ovid's charmer
Who leads the quadrilles in Arcady, boy-lord
Of hearts who can call their Yes and No their own,
Would, madcap that he is, soon die of cold or
sunstroke:
These lives are in firmer hands; that old grim She
Who makes the blind dates for the hatless genera
Creates their country matters. (Woe to the child-bed,
Woe to the strawberries if She's in Her moods!)

And on these attend, greedy as fowl and harsher
Than any climate, Caesar with all his They.
If a tax-collector disappear in the hills,
If, now and then, a keeper is shot in the forest,
No thunder follows, but where roads run level,
How swift to the point of protest strides the Crown.
It hangs, it flogs, it fines, it goes. There is drink.
There are wives to beat. But Zeus is with the strong,

Born as a rule in some small place (an island,
    Quite often, where a smart lad can spot the bluff
Whence cannon would put the harbor at his mercy),
    Though it is here they chamber with Clio. At
                                                this brook
The Christian cross-bow stopped the Heathen scimitar;
    Here is a windmill whence an emperor saw
His right wing crumple; across these cabbage fields
    A pretender's Light Horse made their final charge.

If I were a plainsman I should hate us all,
    From the mechanic rioting for a cheap loaf
To the fastidious palate, hate the painter
    Who steals my wrinkles for his Twelve Apostles,
Hate the priest who cannot even make it shower.
    What could I smile at as I trudged behind my harrow
But bloodshot images of rivers howling,
    Marbles in panic, and Don't-Care made to care?

As it is, though, I know them personally
    Only as a landscape common to two nightmares:
Across them, spotted by spiders from afar,
    I have tried to run, knowing there was no hiding and
                                                no help;

On them, in brilliant moonlight, I have lost my way
    And stood without a shadow at the dead centre
Of an abominable desolation,
    Like Tarquin ravished by his post-coital sadness.

Which goes to show I've reason to be frightened
    Not of plains, of course, but of me. I should like
– Who wouldn't? – to shoot beautifully and be obeyed,
    (I should also like to own a cave with two exits);
I wish I weren't so silly. Though I can't pretend
    To think these flats poetic, it's as well at times
To be reminded that nothing is lovely,
    Not even in poetry, which is not the case.

STREAMS
(for Elizabeth Drew)

Dear water, clear water, playful in all your streams,
as you dash or loiter through life who does not love
    to sit beside you, to hear you and see you,
   pure being, perfect in music and movement?

Air is boastful at times, earth slovenly, fire rude,
but you in your bearing are always immaculate,
    the most well-spoken of all the older
   servants in the household of Mrs Nature.

Nobody suspects you of mocking him, for you still
use the same vocables you were using the day
    before that unexpected row which
   downed every hod on half-finished Babel,

and still talk to yourself: nowhere are you disliked;
arching your torso, you dive from a basalt sill,
    canter across white chalk, slog forward
   through red marls, the aboriginal pilgrim,

at home in all sections, but for whom we should be
idolaters of a single rock, kept apart
    by our landscapes, excluding as alien
   the tales and diets of all other strata.

How could we love the absent one if you did not keep
coming from a distance, or quite directly assist,
 as when past Iseult's tower you floated
 the willow pash-notes of wanted Tristram?

And Homo Ludens, surely, is your child, who make
fun of our feuds by opposing identical banks
 and transferring the loam from Huppim
 to Muppim and back each time you crankle.

Growth cannot add to your song: as unchristened
 brooks
already you whisper to ants what, as Brahma's son,
 descending his titanic staircase
 into Assam, to Himalayan bears you thunder.

And not even man can spoil you: his company
coarsens roses and dogs but, should he
 herd you through a sluice
 to toil at a turbine, or keep you
 leaping in gardens for his amusement,

innocent still is your outcry, water, and there
even, to his soiled heart raging at what it is,
 tells of a sort of world, quite other,
 altogether different from this one

with its envies and passports, a polis like that
to which, in the name of scholars everywhere,
  Gaston Paris pledged his allegiance
 as Bismarck's siege-guns came within earshot.

Lately, in that dale of all Yorkshire's the loveliest,
where, off its fell-side helter-skelter, Kisdon Beck
  jumps into Swale with a boyish shouting,
 sprawled out on grass, I dozed for a second,

and found myself following a croquet tournament
in a calm enclosure, with thrushes popular:
  of all the players in that cool valley
 the best with the mallet was my darling.

While, on the wolds that begirdled it, wild old men
hunted with spades and hammers, monomaniac each,
  for a megalith or a fossil,
 and bird-watchers crept through mossy beech-woods.

Suddenly, over the lawn we started to run
for, lo, through the trees, in a cream and golden coach
  drawn by two baby locomotives,
 the god of mortal doting approached us,

flanked by his bodyguard, those hairy armigers in green
who laugh at thunderstorms and weep at a blue sky:
    He thanked us for our cheers of homage,
  and promised X and Y a passion undying.

With a wave of his torch he commanded a dance;
so round in a ring we flew, my dear on my right,
    when I awoke. But fortunate seemed that
  day because of my dream and enlightened,

and dearer, water, than ever your voice, as if
glad – though goodness knows why – to run with the
                                human race,
    wishing, I thought, the least of men their
  figures of splendor, their holy places.

DEFTLY, ADMIRAL, CAST YOUR FLY

Deftly, admiral, cast your fly
   Into the slow deep hover,
Till the wise old trout mistake and die;
   Salt are the deeps that cover
    The glittering fleets you led,
     White is your head.

Read on, ambassador, engrossed
   In your favorite Stendhal;
The Outer Provinces are lost,
   Unshaven horsemen swill
    The great wines of the Chateaux
     Where you danced long ago.

Do not turn, do not lift your eyes
   Toward the still pair standing
On the bridge between your properties,
   Indifferent to your minding:
    In its glory, in its power,
     This is their hour.

Nothing your strength, your skill, could do
  Can alter their embrace
Or dispersuade the Furies who
  At the appointed place
  With claw and dreadful brow
    Wait for them now.

WHEN RITES AND MELODIES BEGIN

'When rites and melodies begin
   To alter modes and times,
And timid bar-flies boast aloud
   Of uncommitted crimes,
And leading families are proud
   To dine with their black sheep,
What promises, what discipline,
   If any, will Love keep?'
     So roared Fire on their right:
      But Tamino and Pamina
      Walked past its rage,
    Sighing O, sighing O,
   In timeless fermatas of awe and delight
     (Innocent? Yes. Ignorant? No.)
      Down the grim passage.

'When stinking Chaos lifts the latch,
   And Grotte backward spins,
And Helen's nose becomes a beak,
   And cats and dogs grow chins,
And daisies claw and pebbles shriek
   And Form and Color part,
What swarming hatreds then will hatch
   Out of Love's riven heart?'

So hissed Water on their left:
    But Pamina and Tamino
    Opposed its spite,
With his worship, with her sweetness –
O look now! See how they emerge from the cleft
    (Frightened? No. Happy? Yes.)
    Out into sunlight.

MAKE THIS NIGHT LOVEABLE

Make this night loveable,
Moon, and with eye single
Looking down from up there
Bless me, One especial,
And friends everywhere.

With a cloudless brightness
Surround our absences;
Innocent be our sleeps,
Watched by great still spaces,
White hills, glittering deeps.

Parted by circumstance,
Grant each your indulgence
That we may meet in dreams
For talk, for dalliance,
By warm hearths, by cool streams.

Shine lest tonight any,
In the dark suddenly,
Wake alone in a bed
To hear his own fury
Wishing his love were dead.

FIRST THINGS FIRST

Woken, I lay in the arms of my own warmth and
                                            listened
To a storm enjoying its storminess in the winter dark
Till my ear, as it can when half-asleep or half-sober,
Set to work to unscramble that interjectory uproar,
Construing its airy vowels and watery consonants
Into a love-speech indicative of a Proper Name.

Scarcely the tongue I should have chosen, yet, as well
As harshness and clumsiness would allow, it spoke in
                                         your praise,
Kenning you a god-child of the Moon and the
                                       West Wind
With power to tame both real and imaginary monsters,
Likening your poise of being to an upland county,
Here green on purpose, there pure blue for luck.

Loud though it was, alone as it certainly found me,
It reconstructed a day of peculiar silence
When a sneeze could be heard a mile off, and had me
                                         walking
On a headland of lava beside you, the occasion as ageless
As the stare of any rose, your presence exactly
So once, so valuable, so there, so now.

168

This, moreover, at an hour when only too often
A smirking devil annoys me in beautiful English,
Predicting a world where every sacred location
Is a sand-buried site all cultured Texans do,
Misinformed and thoroughly fleeced by their guides,
And gentle hearts are extinct like Hegelian Bishops.

Grateful, I slept till a morning that would not say
How much it believed of what I said the storm had said
But quietly drew my attention to what had been done
– So many cubic metres the more in my cistern
Against a leonine summer – , putting first things first:
Thousands have lived without love, not one without
                                                        water.

THE MORE LOVING ONE

Looking up at the stars, I know quite well
That, for all they care, I can go to hell,
But on earth indifference is the least
We have to dread from man or beast.

How should we like it were stars to burn
With a passion for us we could not return?
If equal affection cannot be,
Let the more loving one be me.

Admirer as I think I am
Of stars that do not give a damn,
I cannot, now I see them, say
I missed one terribly all day.

Were all stars to disappear or die,
I should learn to look at an empty sky
And feel its total dark sublime,
Though this might take me a little time.

PRECIOUS FIVE

Be patient, solemn nose,
Serve in a world of prose
The present moment well,
Nor surlily contrast
Its brash ill-mannered smell
With grand scents of the past.
That calm enchanted wood,
That grave world where you stood
So gravely at its middle,
Its oracle and riddle,
Has all been altered; now
In anxious times you serve
As bridge from mouth to brow,
An asymmetric curve
Thrust outward from a face
Time-conscious into space,
Whose oddness may provoke
To a mind-saving joke
A mind that would it were
An apathetic sphere:
Point, then, for honor's sake
Up the storm-beaten slope
From memory to hope
The way you cannot take.

Be modest, lively ears,
Spoiled darlings of a stage
Where any caper cheers
The paranoiac mind
Of this undisciplined
And concert-going age,
So lacking in conviction
It cannot take pure fiction,
And what it wants from you
Are rumors partly true;
Before you catch its sickness
Submit your lucky quickness
And levity to rule,
Go back again to school,
Drudge patiently until
No whisper is too much
And your precision such
At any sound that all
Seem natural, not one
Fantastic or banal,
And then do what you will:
Dance with angelic grace,
In ecstasy and fun,
The luck you cannot place.

Be civil, hands; on you
Although you cannot read
Is written what you do
And blows you struck so blindly
In temper or in greed,
Your tricks of long ago,
Eyes, kindly or unkindly,
Unknown to you will know.
Revere those hairy wrists
And leg-of-mutton fists
Which pulverised the trolls
And carved deep Donts in stone,
Great hands which under knolls
Are now disjointed bone,
But what has been has been;
A tight arthritic claw
Or aldermanic paw
Waving about in praise
Of those homeric days
Is impious and obscene:
Grow, hands, into those living
Hands which true hands should be
By making and by giving
To hands you cannot see.

Look, naked eyes, look straight
At all eyes but your own
Lest in a tête-à-tête
Of glances double-crossed,
Both knowing and both known,
Your nakedness be lost;
Rove curiously about
But look from inside out,
Compare two eyes you meet
By dozens on the street,
One shameless, one ashamed,
Too lifeless to be blamed,
With eyes met now and then
Looking from living men,
Which in petrarchan fashion
Play opposite the heart,
Their humor to her passion,
Her nature to their art,
For mutual undeceiving;
True seeing is believing
(What sight can never prove)
There is a world to see:
Look outward, eyes, and love
Those eyes you cannot be.

Praise, tongue, the Earthly Muse
By number and by name
In any style you choose,
For nimble tongues and lame
Have both found favor; praise
Her port and sudden ways,
Now fish-wife and now queen,
Her reason and unreason:
Though freed from that machine,
Praise Her revolving wheel
Of appetite and season
In honor of Another,
The old self you become
At any drink or meal,
That animal of taste,
And of his twin, your brother,
Unlettered, savage, dumb,
Down there below the waist:
Although your style be fumbling,
Half stutter and half song,
Give thanks however bumbling,
Telling for Her dear sake
To whom all styles belong
The truth She cannot make.

Be happy, precious five,
So long as I'm alive
Nor try to ask me what
You should be happy for;
Think, if it helps, of love
Or alcohol or gold,
But do as you are told.
I could (which you cannot)
Find reasons fast enough
To face the sky and roar
In anger and despair
At what is going on,
Demanding that it name
Whoever is to blame:
The sky would only wait
Till all my breath was gone
And then reiterate
As if I wasn't there
That singular command
I do not understand,
Bless what there is for being,
Which has to be obeyed, for
What else am I made for,
Agreeing or disagreeing?

THE SHIELD OF ACHILLES

    She looked over his shoulder
        For vines and olive trees,
    Marble well-governed cities
        And ships upon untamed seas,
    But there on the shining metal
        His hands had put instead
    An artificial wilderness
        And a sky like lead.

A plain without a feature, bare and brown,
    No blade of grass, no sign of neighborhood,
Nothing to eat and nowhere to sit down,
    Yet, congregated on its blankness, stood
    An unintelligible multitude,
A million eyes, a million boots in line,
Without expression, waiting for a sign.

Out of the air a voice without a face
    Proved by statistics that some cause was just
In tones as dry and level as the place:
    No one was cheered and nothing was discussed;
    Column by column in a cloud of dust
They marched away enduring a belief
Whose logic brought them, somewhere else, to grief.

She looked over his shoulder
     For ritual pieties,
White flower-garlanded heifers,
     Libation and sacrifice,
But there on the shining metal
     Where the altar should have been,
She saw by his flickering forge-light
     Quite another scene.

Barbed wire enclosed an arbitrary spot
     Where bored officials lounged (one cracked a joke)
And sentries sweated for the day was hot:
     A crowd of ordinary decent folk
     Watched from without and neither moved nor spoke
As three pale figures were led forth and bound
To three posts driven upright in the ground.

The mass and majesty of this world, all
     That carries weight and always weighs the same
Lay in the hands of others; they were small
     And could not hope for help and no help came:
     What their foes liked to do was done, their shame
Was all the worst could wish; they lost their pride
And died as men before their bodies died.

She looked over his shoulder
    For athletes at their games,
Men and women in a dance
    Moving their sweet limbs
Quick, quick, to music,
    But there on the shining shield
His hands had set no dancing-floor
    But a weed-choked field.

A ragged urchin, aimless and alone,
    Loitered about that vacancy; a bird
Flew up to safety from his well-aimed stone:
    That girls are raped, that two boys knife a third,
    Were axioms to him, who'd never heard
Of any world where promises were kept,
Or one could weep because another wept.

The thin-lipped armorer,
    Hephaestos, hobbled away,
Thetis of the shining breasts
    Cried out in dismay
At what the god had wrought
    To please her son, the strong
Iron-hearted man-slaying Achilles
    Who would not live long.

THE OLD MAN'S ROAD

Across the Great Schism, through our whole landscape,
Ignoring God's Vicar and God's Ape,

Under their noses, unsuspected,
The Old Man's Road runs as it did

When a light subsoil, a simple ore
Were still in vogue: true to His wherefore,

By stiles, gates, hedge-gaps it goes
Over ploughland, woodland, cow meadows,

Past shrines to a cosmological myth
No heretic today would be caught dead with,

Near hill-top rings that were so safe then,
Now stormed easily by small children

(Shepherds use bits in the high mountains,
Hamlets take stretches for Lovers' Lanes),

Then through cities threads its odd way,
Now without gutters, a Thieves' Alley,

Now with green lamp-posts and white curb,
The smart Crescent of a high-toned suburb,

Giving wide berth to an old Cathedral,
Running smack through a new Town Hall,

Unlookable for, by logic, by guess:
Yet some strike it, and are struck fearless.

No life can know it, but no life
That sticks to this course can be made captive,

And who wander with it are not stopped at
Borders by guards of some Theocrat,

Crossing the pass so almost where
His searchlight squints but no closer

(And no further where it might by chance):
So in summer sometimes, without hindrance,

Apotropaically scowling, a tinker
Shuffles past, in the waning year

Potters a coleopterist, poking
Through yellow leaves, and a youth in spring

Trots by after a new excitement,
His true self, hot on the scent.

The Old Man leaves his Road to those
Who love it no less since it lost purpose,

Who never ask what History is up to,
So cannot act as if they knew:

Assuming a freedom its Powers deny,
Denying its Powers, they pass freely.

THE HISTORY OF SCIENCE

All fables of adventure stress
The need for courtesy and kindness:
Without the Helpers none can win
The flaxen-haired Princess.

They look the ones in need of aid,
Yet, thanks to them, the gentle-hearted
Third Brother beds the woken Queen,
While seniors who made

Cantankerous replies to crones
And dogs who begged to share their rations,
Must expiate their pride as daws
Or wind-swept bachelor stones.

Few of a sequel, though, have heard:
Uneasy pedagogues have censored
All written reference to a brother
Younger than the Third.

Soft-spoken as New Moon this Fourth,
A Sun of gifts to all he met with,
But when advised 'Go South a while!',
Smiled 'Thank You!' and turned North,

Trusting some map in his own head,
So never reached the goal intended
(His map, of course, was out) but blundered
On a wonderful instead,

A tower not circular but square,
A treasure not of gold but silver:
He kissed a shorter Sleeper's hand
And stroked her raven hair.

Dare sound Authority confess
That one can err his way to riches,
Win glory by mistake, his dear
Through sheer wrong-headedness?

THE HISTORY OF TRUTH

In that ago when being was believing,
Truth was the most of many credibles,
More first, more always, than a bat-winged lion,
A fish-tailed dog or eagle-headed fish,
The least like mortals, doubted by their deaths.

Truth was their model as they strove to build
A world of lasting objects to believe in,
Without believing earthenware and legend,
Archway and song, were truthful or untruthful:
The Truth was there already to be true.

This while when, practical like paper-dishes,
Truth is convertible to kilowatts,
Our last to do by is an anti-model,
Some untruth anyone can give the lie to,
A nothing no one need believe is there.

HOMAGE TO CLIO

Our hill has made its submission and the green
    Swept on into the north: around me,
From morning to night, flowers duel incessantly,
    Color against color, in combats

Which they all win, and at any hour from some point else
    May come another tribal outcry
Of a new generation of birds who chirp,
    Not for effect but because chirping

Is the thing to do. More lives than I perceive
    Are aware of mine this May morning
As I sit reading a book, sharper senses
    Keep watch on an inedible patch

Of unsatisfactory smell, unsafe as
    So many areas are: to observation
My book is dead, and by observations they live
    In space, as unaware of silence

As Provocative Aphrodite or her twin,
    Virago Artemis, the Tall Sisters
Whose subjects they are. That is
                   why, in their Dual Realm,
    Banalities can be beautiful,

Why nothing is too big or too small or the wrong
    Color, and the roar of an earthquake
Rearranging the whispers of streams a loud sound
    Not a din: but we, at haphazard

And unseasonably, are brought face to face
    By ones, Clio, with your silence. After that
Nothing is easy. We may dream as we wish
    Of phallic pillar or navel-stone

With twelve nymphs twirling about it, but pictures
    Are no help: your silence already is there
Between us and any magical centre
    Where things are taken in hand. Besides,

Are we so sorry? Woken at sun-up to hear
    A cock pronouncing himself himself
Though all his sons had been castrated and eaten,
    I was glad I could be unhappy: if

I don't know how I shall manage, at least I know
    The beast-with-two-backs may be a species
Evenly distributed but Mum and Dad
    Were not two other people. To visit

The grave of a friend, to make an ugly scene,
    To count the loves one has grown out of,
Is not nice, but to chirp like a tearless bird,
    As though no one dies in particular

And gossip were never true, unthinkable:
    If it were, forgiveness would be no use,
One-eye-for-one would be just and the innocent
    Would not have to suffer. Artemis,

Aphrodite, are Major Powers and all wise
    Castellans will mind their p's and q's,
But it is you, who never have spoken up,
    Madonna of silences, to whom we turn

When we have lost control, your eyes, Clio, into which
    We look for recognition after
We have been found out. How shall I describe you? They
    Can be represented in granite

(One guesses at once from the perfect buttocks,
    The flawless mouth too grand to have corners,
Whom the colossus must be), but what icon
    Have the arts for you, who look like any

Girl one has not noticed and show no special
    Affinity with a beast? I have seen
Your photo, I think, in the papers, nursing
    A baby or mourning a corpse: each time

You had nothing to say and did not, one could see,
    Observe where you were, Muse of the unique
Historical fact, defending with silence
    Some world of your beholding, a silence

No explosion can conquer but a lover's Yes
    Has been known to fill. So few of the Big
Ever listen: that is why you have a great host
    Of superfluous screams to care for and

Why, up and down like the Duke of Cumberland,
    Or round and round like the Laxey Wheel,
The Short, The Bald, The Pious, The Stammerer went,
    As the children of Artemis go,

Not yours. Lives that obey you move like music,
    Becoming now what they only can be once,
Making of silence decisive sound: it sounds
    Easy, but one must find the time. Clio,

Muse of Time, but for whose merciful silence
  Only the first step would count and that
Would always be murder, whose kindness never
  Is taken in, forgive our noises

And teach us our recollections: to throw away
  The tiniest fault of someone we love
Is out of the question, says Aphrodite,
  Who should know, yet one has known people

Who have done just that. Approachable as you seem,
  I dare not ask you if you bless the poets,
For you do not look as if you ever read them,
  Nor can I see a reason why you should.

THE LOVE FEAST

In an upper room at midnight
See us gathered on behalf
Of love according to the gospel
Of the radio-phonograph.

Lou is telling Anne what Molly
Said to Mark behind her back;
Jack likes Jill who worships George
Who has the hots for Jack.

Catechumens make their entrance;
Steep enthusiastic eyes
Flicker after tits and baskets;
Someone vomits; someone cries.

Willy cannot bear his father,
Lilian is afraid of kids;
The Love that rules the sun and stars
Permits what He forbids.

Adrian's pleasure-loving dachshund
In a sinner's lap lies curled;
Drunken absent-minded fingers
Pat a sinless world.

Who is Jenny lying to
In her call, Collect, to Rome?
The Love that made her out of nothing
Tells me to go home.

But that Miss Number in the corner
Playing hard to get....
I am sorry I'm not sorry ...
Make me chaste, Lord, but not yet.

LIMBO CULTURE

The tribes of Limbo, travellers report,
On first encounter seem much like ourselves;
They keep their houses practically clean,
Their watches round about a standard time,
They serve you almost appetising meals:
But no one says he saw a Limbo child.

The language spoken by the tribes of Limbo
Has many words far subtler than our own
To indicate how much, how little, something
Is pretty closely or not quite the case,
But none you could translate by *Yes* or *No,*
Nor do its pronouns distinguish between Persons.

In tales related by the tribes of Limbo,
Dragon and Knight set to with fang and sword
But miss their rival always by a hair's-breadth,
Old Crone and Stripling pass a crucial point,
She seconds early and He seconds late,
A magic purse mistakes the legal tender:

'And so,' runs their concluding formula,
'Prince and Princess are nearly married still.'
Why this concern, so marked in Limbo culture,
This love for inexactness? Could it be
A Limbo tribesman only loves himself?
For that, we know, cannot be done exactly.

NUMBERS AND FACES

The Kingdom of Number is all boundaries
Which may be beautiful and must be true;
To ask if it is big or small proclaims one
The sort of lover who should stick to faces.

Lovers of small numbers go benignly potty,
Believe all tales are thirteen chapters long,
Have animal doubles, carry pentagrams,
Are Millerites, Baconians, Flat-Earth-Men.

Lovers of big numbers go horridly mad,
Would have the Swiss abolished, all of us
Well purged, somatotyped, baptised, taught baseball:
They empty bars, spoil parties, run for Congress.

True, between faces almost any number
Might come in handy, and One is always real;
But which could any face call good, for calling
Infinity a number does not make it one.

PRIME

Simultaneously, as soundlessly,
  Spontaneously, suddenly
As, at the vaunt of the dawn, the kind
  Gates of the body fly open
To its world beyond, the gates of the mind,
  The horn gate and the ivory gate
Swing to, swing shut, instantaneously
  Quell the nocturnal rummage
Of its rebellious fronde, ill-favored,
  Ill-natured and second-rate,
Disenfranchised, widowed and orphaned
  By an historical mistake:
Recalled from the shades to be a seeing being,
  From absence to be on display,
Without a name or history I wake
  Between my body and the day.

Holy this moment, wholly in the right,
  As, in complete obedience
To the light's laconic outcry, next
  As a sheet, near as a wall,
Out there as a mountain's poise of stone,
  The world is present, about,
And I know that I am, here, not alone
  But with a world and rejoice

Unvexed, for the will has still to claim
    This adjacent arm as my own,
The memory to name me, resume
    Its routine of praise and blame,
And smiling to me is this instant while
    Still the day is intact, and I
The Adam sinless in our beginning,
    Adam still previous to any act.

I draw breath; that is of course to wish
    No matter what, to be wise,
To be different, to die and the cost,
    No matter how, is Paradise
Lost of course and myself owing a death:
    The eager ridge, the steady sea,
The flat roofs of the fishing village
    Still asleep in its bunny,
Though as fresh and sunny still, are not friends
    But things to hand, this ready flesh
No honest equal, but my accomplice now,
    My assassin to be, and my name
Stands for my historical share of care
    For a lying self-made city,
Afraid of our living task, the dying
    Which the coming day will ask.

NONES

What we know to be not possible,
   Though time after time foretold
By wild hermits, by shaman and sybil
   Gibbering in their trances,
Or revealed to a child in some chance rhyme
   Like *will* and *kill*, comes to pass
Before we realize it. We are surprised
   At the ease and speed of our deed
And uneasy: It is barely three,
   Mid-afternoon, yet the blood
Of our sacrifice is already
   Dry on the grass; we are not prepared
For silence so sudden and so soon;
   The day is too hot, too bright, too still,
Too ever, the dead remains too nothing.
   What shall we do till nightfall?

The wind has dropped and we have lost our public.
   The faceless many who always
Collect when any world is to be wrecked,
   Blown up, burnt down, cracked open,
Felled, sawn in two, hacked through, torn apart,
   Have all melted away. Not one
Of these who in the shade of walls and trees
   Lie sprawled now, calmly sleeping,

Harmless as sheep, can remember why
    He shouted or what about
So loudly in the sunshine this morning;
    All if challenged would reply
– 'It was a monster with one red eye,
    A crowd that saw him die, not I.' –
The hangman has gone to wash, the soldiers to eat:
    We are left alone with our feat.

The Madonna with the green woodpecker,
    The Madonna of the fig-tree,
The Madonna beside the yellow dam,
    Turn their kind faces from us
And our projects under construction,
    Look only in one direction,
Fix their gaze on our completed work:
    Pile-driver, concrete-mixer,
Crane and pick-axe wait to be used again,
    But how can we repeat this?
Outliving our act, we stand where we are,
    As disregarded as some
Discarded artifact of our own,
    Like torn gloves, rusted kettles,
Abandoned branch-lines, worn lop-sided
    Grindstones buried in nettles.

This mutilated flesh, our victim,
   Explains too nakedly, too well,
The spell of the asparagus garden,
   The aim of our chalk-pit game; stamps,
Birds' eggs are not the same, behind the wonder
   Of tow-paths and sunken lanes,
Behind the rapture on the spiral stair,
   We shall always now be aware
Of the deed into which they lead, under
   The mock chase and mock capture,
The racing and tussling and splashing,
   The panting and the laughter,
Be listening for the cry and stillness
   To follow after: wherever
The sun shines, brooks run, books are written,
   There will also be this death.

Soon cool tramontana will stir the leaves,
   The shops will re-open at four,
The empty blue bus in the empty pink square
   Fill up and depart: we have time
To misrepresent, excuse, deny,
   Mythify, use this event
While, under a hotel bed, in prison,
   Down wrong turnings, its meaning

200

Waits for our lives. Sooner than we would choose
    Bread will melt, water will burn,
And the great quell begin, Abaddon
    Set up his triple gallows
At our seven gates, fat Belial make
    Our wives waltz naked; meanwhile
It would be best to go home, if we have a home,
    In any case good to rest.

That our dreaming wills may seem to escape
    This dead calm, wander instead
On knife edges, on black and white squares,
    Across moss, baize, velvet, boards,
Over cracks and hillocks, in mazes
    Of string and penitent cones,
Down granite ramps and damp passages,
    Through gates that will not relatch
And doors marked *Private*, pursued by Moors
    And watched by latent robbers,
To hostile villages at the heads of fjords,
    To dark chateaux where wind sobs
In the pine-trees and telephones ring,
    Inviting trouble, to a room,
Lit by one weak bulb, where our Double sits
    Writing and does not look up.

That, while we are thus away, our own wronged flesh
    May work undisturbed, restoring
The order we try to destroy, the rhythm
    We spoil out of spite: valves close
And open exactly, glands secrete,
    Vessels contract and expand
At the right moment, essential fluids
    Flow to renew exhausted cells,
Not knowing quite what has happened, but awed
    By death like all the creatures
Now watching this spot, like the hawk looking down
    Without blinking, the smug hens
Passing close by in their pecking order,
    The bug whose view is balked by grass,
Or the deer who shyly from afar
    Peer through chinks in the forest.

COMPLINE

Now, as desire and the things desired
    Cease to require attention,
As, seizing its chance, the body escapes,
    Section by section, to join
Plants in their chaster peace which is more
    To its real taste, now a day is its past,
Its last deed and feeling in, should come
    The instant of recollection
When the whole thing makes sense: it comes, but all
    I recall are doors banging,
Two housewives scolding, an old man gobbling,
    A child's wild look of envy,
Actions, words, that could fit any tale,
    And I fail to see either plot
Or meaning; I cannot remember
    A thing between noon and three.

Nothing is with me now but a sound,
    A heart's rhythm, a sense of stars
Leisurely walking around, and both
    Talk a language of motion
I can measure but not read: maybe
    My heart is confessing her part
In what happened to us from noon till three,
    That constellations indeed

Sing of some hilarity beyond
    All liking and happening,
But, knowing I neither know what they know
    Nor what I ought to know, scorning
All vain fornications of fancy,
    Now let me, blessing them both
For the sweetness of their cassations,
    Accept our separations.

A stride from now will take me into dream,
    Leave me, without a status,
Among its unwashed tribes of wishes
    Who have no dances and no jokes
But a magic cult to propitiate
    What happens from noon till three,
Odd rites which they hide from me – should I chance,
    Say, on youths in an oak-wood
Insulting a white deer, bribes nor threats
    Will get them to blab – and then,
Past untruth is one step to nothing,
    For the end, for me as for cities,
Is total absence: what comes to be
    Must go back into non-being
For the sake of the equity, the rhythm
    Past measure or comprehending.

Can poets (can men in television)
    Be saved? It is not easy
To believe in unknowable justice
    Or pray in the name of a love
Whose name one's forgotten: *libera*
    Me, libera C (dear C)
And all poor s-o-b's who never
    Do anything properly, spare
Us in the youngest day when all are
    Shaken awake, facts are facts,
(And I shall know exactly what happened
    Today between noon and three)
That we, too, may come to the picnic
    With nothing to hide, join the dance
As it moves in perichoresis,
    Turns about the abiding tree.

FRIDAY'S CHILD

(In memory of Dietrich Bonhoeffer, martyred at Flossenburg, April 9th, 1945)

He told us we were free to choose
But, children as we were, we thought –
'Paternal Love will only use
    Force in the last resort

On those too bumptious to repent.' –
Accustomed to religious dread,
It never crossed our minds He meant
    Exactly what He said.

Perhaps He frowns, perhaps He grieves,
But it seems idle to discuss
If anger or compassion leaves
    The bigger bangs to us.

What reverence is rightly paid
To a Divinity so odd
He lets the Adam whom He made
    Perform the Acts of God?

It might be jolly if we felt
Awe at this Universal Man
(When kings were local, people knelt);
    Some try to, but who can?

The self-observed observing Mind
We meet when we observe at all
Is not alarming or unkind
    But utterly banal.

Though instruments at Its command
Make wish and counterwish come true,
It clearly cannot understand
    What It can clearly do.

Since the analogies are rot
Our senses based belief upon,
We have no means of learning what
    Is really going on,

And must put up with having learned
All proofs or disproofs that we tender
Of His existence are returned
    Unopened to the sender.

Now, did He really break the seal
And rise again? We dare not say;
But conscious unbelievers feel
   Quite sure of Judgement Day.

Meanwhile, a silence on the cross,
As dead as we shall ever be,
Speaks of some total gain or loss,
   And you and I are free

To guess from the insulted face
Just what Appearances He saves
By suffering in a public place
   A death reserved for slaves.

THE CAVE OF MAKING
(In Memoriam Louis MacNeice)

For this and for all enclosures like it the archetype
    is Weland's Stithy, an antre
more private than a bedroom even, for neither lovers nor
    maids are welcome, but without a
bedroom's secrets: from the Olivetti Portable,
    the dictionaries (the very
best money can buy), the heaps of paper, it is evident
    what must go on. Devoid of
flowers and family photographs, all is subordinate
    here to a function, designed to
discourage day-dreams – hence windows
                        averted from plausible
    videnda but admitting a light one
could mend a watch by – and to sharpen hearing:
      reached by an
    outside staircase, domestic
noises and odors, the vast background of natural
    life are shut off. Here silence
is turned into objects.
            I wish, Louis, I could have shown it you
    while you were still in public,
and the house and garden: lover of women and Donegal,

from your perspective you'd notice
sights I overlook, and in turn take a scholar's interest
    in facts I could tell you (for instance,
four miles to our east, at a wood palisade, Carolingian
    Bavaria stopped, beyond it
unknowable nomads). Friends we became by personal
    choice, but fate had already
made us neighbors. For Grammar we both inherited
    good mongrel barbarian English
which never completely succumbed

                                to the Roman rhetoric
    or the Roman gravity, that nonsense
which stood none. Though neither
                        of our dads, like Horace's,
    wiped his nose on his forearm,
neither was porphyry-born, and our ancestors probably
    were among those plentiful subjects
it cost less money to murder. Born so, both of us
    became self-conscious at a moment
when locomotives were named after knights in Malory,
    Science to schoolboys was known as
Stinks, and the Manor still was politically numinous:
    both watched with mixed feelings
the sack of Silence, the churches empty, the cavalry
    go, the Cosmic Model
become German, and any faith, if we had it, in immanent

virtue died. More than ever
life-out-there is goodly, miraculous, loveable,
    but we shan't, not since Stalin and Hitler,
trust ourselves ever again: we know that, subjectively,
    all is possible.
                    To you, though,
ever since, last Fall, you quietly slipped out of Granusion,
    our moist garden, into
the Country of Unconcern, no possibility
    matters. I wish you hadn't
caught that cold, but the dead we miss are easier
    to talk to: with those no longer
tensed by problems one cannot feel shy and, anyway,
    when playing cards or drinking
or pulling faces are out of the question, what else is there
    to do but talk to the voices
of conscience they have become? From
                        now on, as a visitor
    who needn't be met at the station,
your influence is welcome at any hour in my ubity,
    especially here, where titles
from *Poems* to *The Burning Perch* offer proof positive
    of the maker you were, with whom I
once collaborated, once at a weird Symposium
    exchanged winks as a juggins

went on about Alienation.
                              Who would, for preference,
    be a bard in an oral culture,
obliged at drunken feasts to improvise a eulogy
    of some beefy illiterate burner,
giver of rings, or depend for bread on the moods of a
    Baroque Prince, expected,
like his dwarf, to amuse? After all, it's rather a privilege
    amid the affluent traffic
to serve this unpopular art which cannot be turned into
    background-noise for study
or hung as a status-trophy by rising executives,
    cannot be 'done' like Venice
or abridged like Tolstoy, but stubbornly still
                              insists upon
    being read or ignored: our handful
of clients at least can rune. (It's heartless to forget about
    the under-developed countries,
but a starving ear is as deaf as a suburban optimist's:
    to stomachs only the Hindu
integers truthfully speak.) Our forerunners might envy us
    our remnant still able to listen:
as Nietzsche said they would, the *plebs* have got steadily

denser, the *optimates*
quicker still on the uptake. (To-day, even Talleyrand
    might seem a naïf: he had so
little to cope with.) I should like to become, if possible,
    a minor atlantic Goethe,
with his passion for weather and stones
                              but without his silliness
    re the Cross: at times a bore, but,
while knowing Speech can at best, a shadow echoing
    the silent light, bear witness
to the Truth it is not, he wished it were, as the francophil
    gaggle of pure songsters
are too vain to. We're not musicians: to stink of Poetry
    is unbecoming, and never
to be dull shows a lack of taste. Even a limerick
    ought to be something a man of
honor, awaiting death from cancer or a firing-squad,
    could read without contempt: (at
that frontier I wouldn't dare speak to anyone
    in either a prophet's bellow
or a diplomat's whisper.)
                      Seeing you know our mystery
    from the inside and therefore
how much, in our lonely dens, we need the
    companionship
    of our good dead, to give us

comfort on dowly days when the self is a nonentity
   dumped on a mound of nothing,
to break the spell of our
                self-enchantment when lip-smacking
  imps of mawk and hooey
write with us what they will, you
               won't think me imposing if
  I ask you to stay at my elbow
until cocktail-time: dear Shade, for your elegy
  I should have been able to manage
something more like you than this
             egocentric monologue,
  but accept it for friendship's sake.

THE GEOGRAPHY
OF THE HOUSE
(for Christopher Isherwood)

Seated after breakfast
In this white-tiled cabin
Arabs call *The House where
Everybody goes,*
Even melancholics
Raise a cheer to Mrs
Nature for the primal
Pleasures She bestows.

Sex is but a dream to
Seventy-and-over,
But a joy proposed un-
-til we start to shave:
Mouth-delight depends on
Virtue in the cook, but
This She guarantees from
Cradle unto grave.

Lifted off the potty,
Infants from their mothers
Hear their first impartial
Words of worldly praise:
Hence, to start the morning
With a satisfactory
Dump is a good omen
All our adult days.

Revelation came to
Luther in a privy
(Cross-words have been solved there):
Rodin was no fool
When he cast his Thinker,
Cogitating deeply,
Crouched in the position
Of a man at stool.

All the Arts derive from
This ur-act of making,
Private to the artist:
Makers' lives are spent
Striving in their chosen
Medium to produce a
De-narcissus-ised en-
-during excrement.

Freud did not invent the
Constipated miser:
Banks have letter-boxes
Built in their façade
Marked *For Night Deposits*,
Stocks are firm or liquid,
Currencies of nations
Either soft or hard.

Global Mother, keep our
Bowels of compassion
Open through our lifetime,
Purge our minds as well:
Grant us a kind ending,
Not a second childhood,
Petulant, weak-sphinctered,
In a cheap hotel.

Keep us in our station:
When we get pound-noteish,
When we seem about to
Take up Higher Thought,
Send us some deflating
Image like the pained ex-
-pression on a Major
Prophet taken short.

(Orthodoxy ought to
Bless our modern plumbing:
Swift and St Augustine
Lived in centuries
When a stench of sewage
Ever in the nostrils
Made a strong debating
Point for Manichees.)

Mind and Body run on
Different time-tables:
Not until our morning
Visit here can we
Leave the dead concerns of
Yesterday behind us,
Face with all our courage
What is now to be.

THE CAVE OF NAKEDNESS
(for Louis and Emmie Kronenberger)

Don Juan needs no bed, being far too impatient
                  to undress,
nor do Tristan and Isolda, much too in love to care
    for so mundane a matter, but unmythical
mortals require one, and prefer to take their clothes off,
    if only to sleep. That is why bedroom farces
must be incredible to be funny, why Peeping Toms
    are never praised, like novelists or bird-watchers,
for their keenness of observation: where there's a bed,
    be it a nun's restricted cot or an Emperor's
baldachined and nightly-redamselled couch,
                        there are no
    effable data. (Dreams may be repeatable,
but our deeds of errantry in the wilderness of wish
    so often turn out, when told, to be less romantic
that our day's routine: besides, we cannot describe them
    without faking.) Lovers don't see their embraces
as a viable theme for debate, nor a monk his prayers
    (do they, in fact, remember them?): O's of passion,
interior acts of attention, not being a story
    in which the names don't matter but the way
                        of telling,
with a lawyer's wit or a nobleman's assurance,

    does, need a drawing-room of their own. Bed-
                              sitting-rooms
soon drive us crazy, a dormitory even sooner
   turns us to brutes: bona fide architects know
that doors are not emphatic enough, and interpose,
   as a march between two realms, so alien, so disjunct,
the no-man's-land of a stair. The switch from
                           personage,
   with a state number, a first and family name,
to the naked Adam or Eve, and vice versa,
   should not be off-hand or abrupt: a stair retards it
to a solemn procession.
                    Since my infantile entrance
   at my mother's bidding into Edwardian England,
I have suffered the transit over forty thousand times,
   usually, to my chagrin, by myself: about
blended flesh, those midnight colloquia of Darbies
                         and Joans,
   I know nothing therefore, about certain occult
antipathies perhaps too much. Some perks belong,
                         though,
   to all unwilling celibates: our rooms are seldom
battlefields, we enjoy the pleasure of reading in bed
   (as we grow older, it's true, we may find it prudent
to get nodding drunk first), we retain the right
                         to choose
our sacred image. (That I often start with sundry

splendors at sundry times greened after, but always end
    aware of one, the same one, may be of no importance,
but I hope it is.) Ordinary human unhappiness
    is life in its natural color, to cavil
putting on airs: at day-wester to think of nothing
    benign to memorise is as rare as feeling
no personal blemish, and Age, despite its damage,
    is well-off. When they look in their bedroom mirrors,
Fifty-plus may be bored, but Seventeen is faced by
    a frowning failure, with no money, no mistress,
no manner of his own, who never got to Italy
    nor met a great one: to say a few words at banquets,
to attend a cocktail-party in honor of N or M,
    can be severe, but Junior has daily to cope
with ghastly family meals, with dear Papa and Mama
    being odd in the wrong way. (It annoys him to speak,
and it hurts him not to.)
                    When I disband from the world,
    and entrust my future to the Gospel-Makers,
I need not fear (not in neutral Austria) being called for
    in the waist of the night by deaf agents, never
to be heard of on earth again: the assaults I would
                                                    be spared

are none of them princely – fire, nightmare,
                              insomnia's
Vision of Hell, when Nature's wholesome genial fabric
    lies utterly discussed and from a sullen vague
wafts a contagious stench, her adamant minerals
    all corrupt, each life a worthless iteration
of the general loathing (to know that, probably,
    its cause is chemical can degrade the panic,
not stint it). As a rule, with pills to help them,
                              the Holy Four
    exempt my nights from nuisance, and even wake me
when I would be woken, when, audible here and there
    in the half-dark, members of an avian orchestra
are already softly noodling, limbering up for
    an overture at sunrise, their effort to express
in the old convention they inherit that joy in beginning
    for which our species was created, and declare it
good. We may not be obliged – though it is mannerly –
                              to bless
    the Trinity that we are corporal contraptions,
but only a villain will omit to thank Our Lady or
    her hen-wife, Dame Kind, as he, she, or both
                              ensemble,
emerge from a private cavity to be re-born,
    re-neighbored in the Country of Consideration.

THE COMMON LIFE
(for Chester Kallman)

A living-room, the catholic area you
    (Thou, rather) and I may enter
without knocking, leave without a bow, confronts
    each visitor with a style,

a secular faith: he compares its dogmas
    with his, and decides whether
he would like to see more of us. (Spotless rooms
    where nothing's left lying about

chill me, so do cups used for ash-trays or smeared
    with lip-stick: the homes I warm to,
though seldom wealthy, always convey a feeling
    of bills being promptly settled

with cheques that don't
               bounce.) There's no *We* at an instant,
    only *Thou* and *I*, two regions
of protestant being which nowhere overlap:
    a room is too small, therefore,

if its occupants cannot forget at will
    that they are not alone, too big
if it gives them any excuse in a quarrel
    for raising their voices. What,

quizzing ours, would Sherlock Holmes infer? Plainly,
    ours is a sitting culture
in a generation which prefers comfort
    (or is forced to prefer it)

to command, would rather incline its buttocks
    on a well-upholstered chair
than the burly back of a slave: a quick glance
    at book-titles would tell him

that we belong to the clerisy and spend much
    on our food. But could he read
what our prayers and jokes are about, what creatures
    frighten us most, or what names

head our roll-call of persons we would least like
    to go to bed with? What draws
singular lives together in the first place,
    loneliness, lust, ambition,

or mere convenience, is obvious, why they drop
   or murder one another
clear enough: how they create, though, a common world
   between them, like Bombelli's

impossible yet useful numbers, no one
   has yet explained. Still, they do
manage to forgive impossible behavior,
   to endure by some miracle

conversational tics and larval habits
   without wincing (were you to die,
I should miss yours). It's a wonder that neither
   has been butchered by accident,

or, as lots have, silently vanished into
   History's criminal noise
unmourned for, but that, after twenty-four years,
   we should sit here in Austria

as cater-cousins, under the glassy look
   of a Naples Bambino,
the portrayed regards of Strauss and Stravinsky,
   doing British cross-word puzzles,

is very odd indeed. I'm glad the builder gave
    our common-room small windows
through which no observed outsider can observe us:
    every home should be a fortress,

equipped with all the very latest engines
    for keeping Nature at bay,
versed in all ancient magic, the arts of quelling
    the Dark Lord and his hungry

animivorous chimaeras. (Any brute
    can buy a machine in a shop,
but the sacred spells are secret to the kind,
    and if power is what we wish

they won't work.) *The ogre will come in any case*:
    so Joyce has warned us. Howbeit,
fasting or feasting, we both know this: without
    the Spirit we die, but life

without the Letter is in the worst of taste,
    and always, though truth and love
can never really differ, when they seem to,
    the subaltern should be truth.

A CHANGE OF AIR

Corns, heartburn, sinus headaches, such minor ailments
Tell of estrangement between your name and you,
Advise a change of air: heed them, but let
The modesty of their discomfort warn you
Against the flashy errands of your dreams.

To grow a sailor's beard, don monkish garb,
Or trade in an agglutinative tongue
With a stone-age culture, would be molly-coddling:
To go Elsewhere is to withdraw from movement;
A side-step, a short one, will convey you thither.

Although its chaffinches, maybe, have learned
The dialect of another river-basin,
A fault transformed the local building stone,
It has a priest, a post-mistress, an usher,
Its children know they are not to beg from strangers.

Within its average elsewhereishness
Your name is as a mirror answers, yourself
How you behave in shops, the tips you give:
It sides with neither, being outside both,
But welcomes both with healing disregard.

Nor, when you both return here (for you will)
Where luck and instinct originally brought you,
Will it salute your reconciliation
With farewell rites, or populate your absence
With reverent and irreverent anecdote.

No study of your public re-appearance
Will show, as judgement on a cure demands,
A sudden change in love, ideas, or diet:
Your sojourn Elsewhere will remain a wordless
Hiatus in your voluble biography.

Fanatic scholarship at most may prove
That you resigned from some Committee, unearth
A letter from the Grand-Duke to his cousin,
Remarking, among more more important gossip,
That you seem less amusing than you were.

ON THE CIRCUIT

Among pelagian travellers,
Lost on their lewd conceited way
To Massachusetts, Michigan,
Miami or L.A.,

An air-borne instrument I sit,
Predestined nightly to fulfil
Columbia-Giesen-Management's
Unfathomable will,

By whose election justified,
I bring my gospel of the Muse
To fundamentalists, to nuns,
To Gentiles and to Jews,

And daily, seven days a week,
Before a local sense has jelled,
From talking-site to talking-site
Am jet-or-prop-propelled.

Though warm my welcome everywhere,
I shift so frequently, so fast,
I cannot now say where I was
The evening before last,

Unless some singular event
Should intervene to save the place,
A truly asinine remark,
A soul-bewitching face,

Or blessed encounter, full of joy,
Unscheduled on the Giesen Plan,
With here, an addict of Tolkien,
There, a Charles Williams fan.

Since Merit but a dunghill is,
I mount the rostrum unafraid:
Indeed, 'twere damnable to ask
If I am overpaid.

Spirit is willing to repeat
Without a qualm the same old talk,
But Flesh is homesick for our snug
Apartment in New York.

A sulky fifty-six, he finds
A change of meal-time utter hell,
Grown far too crotchety to like
A luxury hotel.

The Bible is a goodly book
I always can peruse with zest,

But really cannot say the same
For Hilton's *Be My Guest*,

Nor bear with equanimity
The radio in students' cars,
Muzak at breakfast, or – dear God! –
Girl-organists in bars.

Then, worst of all, the anxious thought,
Each time my plane begins to sink
And the No Smoking sign comes on:
What will there be to drink?

Is this a milieu where I must
How grahamgreeneish! How infra dig!
Snatch from the bottle in my bag
An analeptic swig?

Another morning comes: I see,
Dwindling below me on the plane,
The roofs of one more audience
I shall not see again.

God bless the lot of them, although
I don't remember which was which:
God bless the U.S.A., so large,
So friendly, and so rich.

THE HORATIANS

Into what fictive realms can imagination
translate you, Flaccus, and your kin? Not the courts of
    Grand Opera, that *galère*
    of lunatics, power-famished

or love-ravenous, belting out their arias,
nor the wards of *Buffa*, either, where abnormal
    growths of self-love are excised
    by the crude surgery of a

practical joke. Perhaps the only invented
story in which your appearance seems credible
    is the Whodunit: I can
    believe in one of you solving

a murder which has the professionals baffled,
thanks to your knowledge of local topography.
    In our world all of you share
    a love for some particular

place and stretch of country, a farm near Tivoli
or a Radnorshire village: what the Capital
    holds out as a lure, a chance
    to get into Society,

does not tempt you, who wry from crowds,
                                        traffic-noises,
blue-stockings and millionaires. Your tastes run to
        small dinner-parties, small rooms,
            and the tone of voice that suits them,

neither truckle nor thrasonical but softly
certain (a sound wood-winds imitate better
        than strings), your most worldly wish
            a genteel sufficiency of

land or lolly. Among those I really know, the
British branch of the family, how many have
        found in the Anglican Church
            your Maecenas who enabled

a life without cumber, as pastors adjective
to rustic flocks, as organists in trollopish
        cathedral towns. Then, in all
            labyrinthine economies

there are obscure nooks into which Authority
never pokes a suspicious nose, *embusqué* havens
    for natural bachelors
    and political idiots,

Zoological and Botanical Gardens,
museum-basements displaying feudal armor
    or old coins: there, too, we find
    you among the custodians.

Some of you have written poems, usually
short ones, and some kept diaries, seldom published
    till after your deaths, but most
    make no memorable impact

except on your friends and dogs. Enthusiastic
Youth writes you off as cold, who cannot be found on
    barricades, and never shoot
    either yourselves or your lovers.

You thought well of your Odes,
                        Flaccus, and believed they
would live, but knew, and have
                        taught your descendants to
    say with you: 'As makers go,
    compared with Pindar or any

of the great foudroyant masters who don't ever
amend, we are, for all our polish, of little
stature, and, as human lives,
compared with authentic martyrs

like Regulus, of no account. We can only
do what it seems to us we were made for, look at
this world with a happy eye
but from a sober perspective.'

AUGUST 1968

The Ogre does what ogres can,
Deeds quite impossible for Man,
But one prize is beyond his reach,
The Ogre cannot master Speech.
About a subjugated plain,
Among its desperate and slain,
The Ogre stalks with hands on hips,
While drivel gushes from his lips.

FAIRGROUND

Thumping old tunes give a voice to its whereabouts
long before one can see the dazzling archway
of colored lights, beyond which household proverbs
cease to be valid,

a ground sacred to the god of vertigo
and his cult of disarray: here jeopardy,
panic, shock, are dispensed in measured doses
by fool-proof engines.

As passive objects, packed tightly together
on Roller-Coaster or Ferris-Wheel, mortals
taste in their solid flesh the volitional
joys of a seraph.

Soon the Roundabout ends the clumsy conflict
of Right and Left: the riding mob melts into
one spinning sphere, the perfect shape performing
the perfect motion.

Mopped and mowed at, as their train worms through
                                        a tunnel,
by ancestral spooks, caressed by clammy cobwebs,
grinning initiates emerge into daylight
as tribal heroes.

Fun for Youth who knows his libertine spirit
is not a copy of Father's, but has yet to
learn that the tissues which lend it stamina,
like Mum's, are bourgeois.

Those with their wander-years behind them,
                                    who are rather
relieved that all routes of escape are spied on,
all hours of amusement counted, requiring
caution, agenda,

keep away: – to be found in coigns where, sitting
in silent synods, they play chess or cribbage,
games that call for patience, foresight, manoeuvre,
like war, like marriage.

RIVER PROFILE

Our body is a moulded river
NOVALIS

Out of a bellicose fore-time, thundering
head-on collisions of cloud and rock in an
up-thrust, crevasse-and-avalanche, troll country,
deadly to breathers,

it whelms into our picture below the melt-line,
where tarns lie frore under frowning cirques, goat-bell,
wind-breaker, fishing-rod, miner's-lamp country,
already at ease with

the mien and gestures that become its kindness,
in streams, still anonymous, still jumpable,
flows as it should through any declining country
in probing spirals.

Soon of a size to be named and the cause of
dirty in-fighting among rival agencies,
down a steep stair, penstock-and-turbine country,
it plunges ram-stam,

to foam through a wriggling gorge incised in softer
strata, hemmed between crags that nauntle heaven,
robber-baron, tow-rope, portage-way country,
nightmare of merchants.

Disemboguing from foothills, now in hushed meanders,
now in riffling braids, it vaunts across a senile
plain, well-entered, chateau-and-cider-press country,
its regal progress

gallanted for a while by quibbling poplars,
then by chimneys: led off to cool and launder
retort, steam-hammer, gasometer country,
it changes color.

Polluted, bridged by girders, banked by concrete,
now it bisects a polyglot metropolis,
ticker-tape, taxi, brothel, foot-lights country,
à-la-mode always.

Broadening or burrowing to the moon's phases,
turbid with pulverised wastemantle, on through
flatter, duller, hotter, cotton-gin country
it scours, approaching

the tidal mark where it puts off majesty,
disintegrates, and through swamps of a delta,
punting-pole, fowling-piece, oyster-tongs country,
wearies to its final

act of surrender, effacement, atonement
in a huge amorphous aggregate no cuddled
attractive child ever dreams of, non-country,
image of death as

a spherical dew-drop of life. Unlovely
monsters, our tales believe, can be translated
too, even as water, the selfless mother
of all especials.

OLD PEOPLE'S HOME

All are limitory, but each has her own
nuance of damage. The elite can dress and
                              decent themselves,
  are ambulant with a single stick, adroit
to read a book all through, or play the slow movements of
  easy sonatas. (Yes, perhaps their very
carnal freedom is their spirit's bane: intelligent
  of what has happened and why, they are obnoxious
to a glum beyond tears.) Then come those on
                         wheels, the average
  majority, who endure T.V. and, led by
lenient therapists, do community-singing, then
  the loners, muttering in Limbo, and last
the terminally incompetent, as improvident,
  unspeakable, impeccable as the plants
they parody. (Plants may sweat profusely but never
  sully themselves.) One tie, though, unites them: all
appeared when the world, though much was awry there,
                            was more
  spacious, more comely to look at, its Old Ones
with an audience and secular station. Then a child,
  in dismay with Mamma, could refuge with Gran
to be revalued and told a story. As of now,
  we all know what to expect, but their generation

is the first to fade like this, not at home but assigned
    to a numbered frequent ward, stowed out of conscience
as unpopular luggage.
                    As I ride the subway
    to spend half-an-hour with one, I revisage
who she was in the pomp and sumpture of her hey-day,
    when week-end visits were a presumptive joy,
not a good work. Am I cold to wish for a speedy
    painless dormition, pray, as I know she prays,
that God or Nature will abrupt her earthly function?

LULLABY

The din of work is subdued,
another day has westered
and mantling darkness arrived.
Peace! Peace! Devoid your portrait
of its vexations and rest.
Your daily round is done with,
you've gotten the garbage out,
answered some tiresome letters
and paid a bill by return,
all *frettolosamente*.
Now you have licence to lie,
naked, curled like a shrimplet,
jacent in bed, and enjoy
its cosy micro-climate:
Sing, Big Baby, sing lullay.

The old Greeks got it all wrong:
Narcissus is an oldie,
tamed by time, released at last
from lust for other bodies,
rational and reconciled.
For many years you envied
the hirsute, the he-man type.

No longer: now you fondle
your almost feminine flesh
with mettled satisfaction,
imagining that you are
sinless and all-sufficient,
snug in the den of yourself,
Madonna and *Bambino*:
Sing, Big Baby, sing lullay.

Let your last thinks all be thanks:
praise your parents who gave you
a Super-Ego of strength
that saves you so much bother,
digit friends and dear them all,
then pay fair attribution
to your age, to having been
born when you were. In boyhood
you were permitted to meet
beautiful old contraptions,
soon to be banished from earth,
saddle-tank loks, beam-engines
and over-shot waterwheels.
Yes, love, you have been lucky:
Sing, Big Baby, sing lullay.

Now for oblivion: let
the belly-mind take over
down below the diaphragm,
the domain of the Mothers,
They who guard the Sacred Gates,
without whose wordless warnings
soon the verbalising I
becomes a vicious despot,
lewd, incapable of love,
disdainful, status-hungry.
Should dreams haunt you, heed them not,
for all, both sweet and horrid,
are jokes in dubious taste,
too jejune to have truck with.
Sleep, Big Baby, sleep your fill.

A THANKSGIVING

When pre-pubescent I felt
that moorlands and woodlands were sacred:
   people seemed rather profane.

Thus, when I started to verse,
I presently sat at the feet of
   Hardy and *Thomas* and *Frost.*

Falling in love altered that,
now Someone, at least, was important:
   Yeats was a help, so was *Graves.*

Then, without warning, the whole
Economy suddenly crumbled:
   there, to instruct me, was *Brecht.*

Finally, hair-raising things
that Hitler and Stalin were doing
   forced me to think about God.

Why was I sure they were wrong?
Wild *Kierkegaard, Williams* and *Lewis*
   guided me back to belief.

Now, as I mellow in years
and home in a bountiful landscape,
   Nature allures me again.

Who are the tutors I need?
Well, *Horace*, adroitest of makers,
   beeking in Tivoli, and

Goethe, devoted to stones,
who guessed that – he never could prove it –
   Newton led Science astray.

Fondly I ponder You all:
without You I couldn't have managed
   even my weakest of lines.

ARCHAEOLOGY

The archaeologist's spade
delves into dwellings
vacancied long ago,

unearthing evidence
of life-ways no one
would dream of leading now,

concerning which he has not much
to say that he can prove: —
the lucky man!

Knowledge may have its purposes,
but guessing is always
more fun than knowing.

We do know that Man,
from fear or affection,
has always graved His dead.

What disastered a city,
volcanic effusion,
fluvial outrage,

or a human horde,
agog for slaves and glory,
is visually patent,

and we're pretty sure that,
as soon as palaces were built,
their rulers,

though gluttoned on sex
and blanded by flattery,
must often have yawned.

But do grain-pits signify
a year of famine?
Where a coin-series

peters out, should we infer
some major catastrophe?
Maybe. Maybe.

From murals and statues
we get a glimpse of what
the Old Ones bowed down to,

but cannot conceit
in what situations they blushed
or shrugged their shoulders.

Poets have learned us their myths,
but just how did They take them?
That's a stumper.

When Norsemen heard thunder,
did they seriously believe
Thor was hammering?

No, I'd say: I'd swear
that men have always lounged in myths
as Tall Stories,

that their real earnest
has been to grant excuses
for ritual actions.

Only in rites
can we renounce our oddities
and be truly entired.

Not that all rites
should be equally fonded:
some are abominable.

There's nothing the Crucified
would like less
than butchery to appease Him.

CODA

From Archaeology
one moral, at least, may be drawn,
to wit, that all

our school text-books lie.
What they call History
is nothing to vaunt of,

being made, as it is,
by the criminal in us:
goodness is timeless.

INDEX OF FIRST LINES